RONALD ROOD,
author of the popular *How Do You Spank a Porcupine?*

"In these chatty, cheerful pages, he discourses on . . . snakes, lizards, termites, and skunks. He tells of an unusual household where it's not uncommon to find a snake in your sneakers or a muskrat in the bathtub."
—*Cincinnati Post & Times-Star*

Anything from chicks and tropical fish to skunks and spiders can make fascinating, instructive, and even affectionate members of your household. And in case you don't want to wait for one to join your household by accident, Ronald Rood tells you where to find and capture it.

So, whether you want to keep a flock of pets that can only be seen under the microscope or something more exotic like a skunk or a bird of prey, let Ronald Rood show you how to care for and enjoy them.

**MAY I KEEP THIS CLAM, MOTHER?
IT FOLLOWED ME HOME**
was originally published by Simon and Schuster.

Books by Ronald Rood

How Do You Spank a Porcupine?
May I Keep This Clam, Mother? It Followed Me Home
Wild Brother

Published by POCKET BOOKS

 *Are there paperbound books you want
but cannot find in your retail stores?*

You can get any title in print in **POCKET BOOK** editions. Simply
send retail price, local sales tax, if any, plus 25¢ (50¢ if you
order two or more books) to cover mailing and handling costs to:

MAIL SERVICE DEPARTMENT
POCKET BOOKS • A Division of Simon & Schuster, Inc.
1 West 39th Street • New York, New York 10018

Please send check or money order. We cannot be responsible
for cash.   *Catalogue sent free on request.*

RONALD ROOD

May I Keep This Clam,
Mother?
It Followed Me Home

ILLUSTRATIONS BY
RICHARD AMUNDSEN

PUBLISHED BY POCKET BOOKS NEW YORK

MAY I KEEP THIS CLAM, MOTHER?
IT FOLLOWED ME HOME

Simon and Schuster edition published 1973

POCKET BOOK edition published August, 1976

This POCKET BOOK edition includes every word contained in
the original, higher-priced edition. It is printed from brand-
new plates made from completely reset, clear, easy-to-read type.
POCKET BOOK editions are published by
POCKET BOOKS,
a division of Simon & Schuster, Inc.,
A GULF+WESTERN COMPANY
630 Fifth Avenue,
New York, N.Y. 10020.
Trademarks registered in the United States
and other countries.

ISBN: 0-671-80672-6.
Library of Congress Catalog Card Number: 73-10597.

Printed in the U.S.A.

*To the memory of one small wood turtle
who struggled along on bread and water
because I hadn't yet written
—and read—this book*

Contents

1. So You're Stuck with a Pet...

When the lady growled at my friend in the elevator, he hastily raised his eyes and contemplated the ceiling. Then she barked at him.

He looked at her, startled. "I beg your pardon?"

There were just the two of them in the elevator. By way of explanation, she patted a bulge in the region of her tummy. "Billy," she said.

This didn't exactly clear things up, so she gently eased her coat open and showed him the head of a little dog.

The revelation took my friend aback. Dog's weren't allowed in the apartment building. But the lady seemed surprised, too. "Billy seldom growls," she said, mystified. "And he never barks." Then she peered significantly at my friend's heavy overcoat. "I wonder why he's so upset?"

Now it was my friend's turn. "Perhaps," he countered, "he got wind of little Lilac."

With that he loosened his own coat. Cradled in the hollow between his chest and his arm was a furry bundle the size of a cat. It was glossy black with a white stripe.

"A skunk?" she asked. "Right here in Manhattan?"

"A skunk," he agreed. "Right here in Manhattan."

Her curiosity whetted, the lady continued the conversation, getting off at my friend's door. It seems that he and his family had been enjoying a May weekend in the Adirondacks when they heard a faint chattering at the base of a decaying tree. There, alone with its three dead littermates, was a baby skunk. Blind and almost naked, it was stiff with the cold.

Obviously it had lost its mother. So, despite the foundling's feeble attempts to defend itself with tiny spray guns that were not yet loaded, my friend bundled it up and brought it home with him.

The family experimented to learn how to feed and care for an orphaned woodland waif. Unable to find much information on raising baby skunks, they decided to treat her like a kitten. Their efforts were well rewarded, for Lilac grew to be as friendly and lovable as any household pet.

In answer to the lady's question—and to mine when I first saw the alert, inquisitive creature—Lilac remained an unexpurgated wood pussy, in complete charge of all her faculties. And never once did she see fit to use that powerful weapon left to her by her thoughtful master.

She lived in the apartment building for two years. She went for clandestine walks in a nearby park with some family member before dawn on Sundays, and on stormy nights when a human huddled in a raincoat would be less likely to excite suspicion. She may be with them still, raising an occasional eyebrow among her human neighbors and a muffled yelp from curious canines.

My friend, who must remain anonymous if he is to keep his lease, was lucky. There are thousands, even millions, of one-animal zookeepers who are not so fortunate. They do not know where to turn for help with their pets. And even less fortunate are the birds, beasts, turtles, insects and assorted other creatures, that find themselves under their care.

Perhaps you are one of these people. Perhaps you are like the mother of a boy who gave me the title for this book. My good friend, Mrs. Pat Armstrong, told us around coffee one evening about how her small son, Keith, arrived home from summer camp complete with never-washed sheets, never-worn clothes (except the disreputable ones he had on)—and one very uncommunicative clam. And the clam had indeed "followed" him home, if you don't worry about stretching the truth a little. It had been piled into the trunk of the family car along with other souvenirs, and hence was the last to arrive.

Well, how would *you* care for a clam? Or in case clams are not your dish, how about a nest of sparrows whose mother has been struck down by an automobile? Or a chipmunk orphaned by a cat?

But there are wild creatures other than clams and sparrows and chipmunks; more than a million animal species, in fact, if you count everything from an

11

amoeba to a zebra (although, as we'll see, there's some question as to what you do with an amoeba). For our purposes they are all animals, even if the term "animal" usually brings to mind something warm and furry like a dog or cat.

And speaking of dogs and cats, they'll receive less than top billing in these pages—except as their care applies to wild animals or to nondomestic creatures not usually thought of as pets. It's the care and feeding of unplanned-for pets that concerns us here.

There are hundreds of fine books in print on the subject of domestic pets. But can a book, say, about the English springer spaniel be applied to an orphaned fox pup? A raccoon? Or maybe even a rabbit? And how about in-between creatures—our own current canine, for example, the offspring of a midnight liaison between a half-wolf lead dog on a sled team and one of its running mates. How many pages from the book about the forty-pound springer can be applied to our own Laska, twice that size, for whom no book has been written?

It is because of such puzzling situations that this volume has come into existence. And it has been a long time in the writing. It all started with a question I put to my boyhood idol, Thornton Burgess, more than forty years ago. My father and I found a baby wood turtle wandering on a Connecticut road on Thanksgiving morning. Dad couldn't explain why the turtle wasn't hibernating, so I wrote to Mr. Burgess. What, I asked in my laborious handwriting, was a turtle doing out on such a frosty day? How could I care for him?

The man whose animal stories have enchanted four generations of readers said he didn't understand the event either. However, perhaps the small turtle had been called forth by an unusual warm spell. The best thing to do was to put him back under the stone or

12

rotting log where he had been hibernating. Since the chances of finding that log or stone were small, Mr. Burgess went on, the next best thing was to fashion a box of leaves and soil in the cellar and hope he'd sleep there through the winter.

I followed his instructions, digging a slumber pit the size of a washtub in the dirt floor of our cellar. But, alas, the small turtle had had enough. Pushed further than he could endure by the enthusiastic attention of a seven-year-old boy and all the kids in the neighborhood, he gave up the ghost. When we went to install him in his hibernaculum, his little red legs and black head merely drooped limply out through that tortoiseshell exterior.

Don Brown and Irv Lake and I gave him a solemn funeral in a cereal-box coffin. But his demise was, perhaps, a stroke of luck. Stung by failure, I determined to do better the next time—and the next.

Now, more than forty years and several hundred animals later, I am, indeed, doing better. True, I still have my share of losses—like the wounded golden eagle that was brought to me and for which I cared constantly for six months until she died. Or like the three hundred black widow spiderlings that solved their own food problems by consuming each other while I was away. But in talking with zoo officials, aquarists, veterinarians, farmers, outdoorsmen and pet owners, I have evolved a number of fundamentals of animal care. They work, with variations, for wild and domestic pets alike.

Over the years, in reading nearly everything I could find about animals, I have discovered that there *is* plenty of material in that spaniel book that would apply to Laska—or to Fido, or Spot, or whatever your dog's name may be. Some of it works for skunks, too. The Siamese cat book can be used for raccoons, to some extent, although I can just hear the anguished yowls from outraged cat fanciers. A ten-dollar volume on raising gouramis in a heated aquarium has plenty of tips for your fifty-cent goldfish in its big mayonnaise jar. And your neighbor's Flemish giant rabbit isn't much different from the frightened native bunny plowed up by the bulldozer scraping the site for your new house.

After all, the plushest pedigreed pet is but the swing of a door away from its free-loving, free-living country cousins. To prove it, just try letting your prize-winning Persian cat out the door when the moon is right—and see if you can get a litter of prize-winning Persian kittens! And a game warden once told me that one of the saddest tasks he ever had was that of shooting a Field Trial Triple Champion worth thousands of dollars. The dog's offense? He was caught killing a deer.

Your orphaned chipmunk in his pasteboard box is, except for the lack of an Andean fur parka, more or less a woodland version of the expensive chinchilla in its air-conditioned cage. And they both have many of the same needs as the gerbil or the hamster—or, for that matter, the brood of common rats that a small correspondent in Chicago wrote me about.

These rats, by the way—if you can control your shudders long enough to let me tell you more—made fine pets for my pen pal and his family. He had got them while they were pink and blind and helpless, and they looked to him as a sort of mother. It was a sorrowful day when they chewed their way out through the cage and escaped—doubtless right into the gleeful clutches of some cat in the alley behind the house.

One other point. And this, I believe, is reason enough for the existence of this book—even though I wish the facts were otherwise. It has to do with a telephone call from Norman, Oklahoma.

It seems that nearly all of us have an urge to collect

15

and fuss over something, whether it's a painting by an old master or a dime-store turtle. And the lady who called long distance that June morning was turning to me for help with her own special collection: three baby starlings. How, she wondered, could she best take care of them?

I considered the habits of this feathered immigrant from the Old World. I recalled the pushy ways of one starling who disregarded the cries of a pair of blue-birds as he and his mate muscled in and built a nest right on top of the bluebirds' helpless young. I pic-tured public buildings whitewashed by his droppings, and small birds fleeing as he and his rowdy pals de-scended on a winter feeder in a greedy, discourteous rabble.

Why couldn't the woman have found a couple of dodos, perhaps, or at least an orphaned whooping crane? Now, *they'd* be worth a person-to-person call from Oklahoma to Vermont. But starlings?

Fortunately my flippant remarks died before I had a chance to utter them. Somewhere a little voice made itself heard:

Now, wait a minute, it said. Norman, Oklahoma, is not Lincoln, Vermont. It's a city. And this woman may live four stories up, right in the heart of it. May-be those young starlings, bent on self-preservation, represent her only link with the world of nature.

And, indeed, this was largely true. Her single win-dow, I learned, faced across the street to the window of another city dweller. The rest of her outlook con-sisted of cement and taxicabs and the lonesome light in the hall. Those starlings, clinging to the grating of her fire escape, were as important to her as twin fawns in a forest would be to me.

I gave her a few suggestions over the phone. Then I sat down and typed her a long letter. Sent it Air

16

Mail Special Delivery, too, so it would get there in time.

You'll find part of her letter in this book. You may not recognize it, because some of it is in one of the chapters on mammals, some is in earthworms, and there's even a bit in the section on frogs.

Perhaps you, too, have a splendid view of the gentleman across the street as he sits and watches television. And possibly you are struggling with your own version of three baby starlings—or a stray kitten, perhaps, or a caterpillar you found in the park. Maybe you are staring helplessly at one of the most forlorn bits of life on this earth: an Easter duckling, dyed blue, and presented by Aunt Diapason to your three delirious children in a rare fit of misguided judgment. What on earth do you do now?

Of course, you can open this book. In it you will find suggestions on what to do when Tabby presents you with a mussed-up baby blackbird, or when Prentiss comes home from school with Something that keeps making his pocket change shape while he explains how he got It for only a jackknife and two ballpoint pens.

And who knows? When Junior arrives home from camp, you, too, may become the foster parent of a recalcitrant clam. Such an event could be downright traumatic, or it could be the highlight of an entire summer. Really.

And on the subject of clams, by the way, I can speak with ringing authority. I had fourteen of them for more than two years.

2. Horse Sense, Common Sense and T.L.C.

Every autumn it's the same. The telephone rings, I answer it, and for the next ten minutes I'm right in the middle of someone else's pet troubles.

I look forward to these phone calls. I appreciate being asked to help, although there's usually little real aid to offer. The details may vary from call to call, but the problem is an old, familiar one. In fact, I suspect it antedates the telephone by a million years, more or less, depending on when man first brought a wolf cub to his cave.

The trouble, simply, is that kittens grow up into cats. And puppies turn into dogs. And, as the party on the other end of the telephone has discovered, small woods creatures get to be large ones.

Sometimes the problem child in question is a raccoon. Last spring, the story might go, someone discovered the youngster with the dark mask and the exploring, almost-human hands and brought him home. There he shared the family's warmth and affection—often its bed and board, too, as raccoons eat almost anything a human will eat, and will readily snuggle down between the sheets with some lucky family member. In fact, Scamper, our first raccoon, used to burrow to the bottom of the sleeping bag of one of my small descendants. And there she would stay without a breath of fresh air until morning.

Little raccoons are amusing, yes. They are downright fascinating. So are large raccoons. But now that it's September, something new is added. Cute little Ricky becomes independent. Instead of coming when you call, he scurries up into a tree. He rips up your good fall coat for bedding, scorning the box of old rags that served him all summer. And when you try to chastise him for filching that hot dog off the picnic table, he whirls and bites you.

And so the question: Do I know of anyone who would take over Ricky and his problems? The problems aren't mentioned, of course, for which I can hardly blame the caller. When I say that I know of nobody willing to inherit such an active bag of tricks, the next question follows: "Well then, Mr. Rood, could you take him out in the woods someplace and give him his freedom?"

And there it is. Kittens into cats. Little wild animals

into bigger ones—whether the problem is raccoons, skunks, squirrels, or even hand-raised native birds. Last spring it was only human for your heart to go out to that baby who was so alone in the world. It was also human to hope that little Rufus, the wildcat, would grow up to be like his domestic cousins rather than like his mother and father. 'Tain't so, of course. And when the bubble bursts, my phone rings.

I cannot lecture those distraught folks on the telephone. But whenever I can buttonhole people, whether it's several hundred captive kids at a school assembly or half a dozen parents at a P.T.A. meeting, I try to stress a few points about pets that, I believe, will cure as many headaches as a bucket of aspirin.

To begin with, there are far fewer orphan wildlings than people seem to believe. Just because you find a young robin or a baby rabbit wobbling along without any parental guidance it is no sign that you are automatically elected to be its mother. Chances are that the mother is away on business of her own. If she leaves her youngster alone except to attend to his basic needs, it may be because her large presence might attract unnecessary visitors. Not only that, but the baby must learn to fend for itself. Unless, of course, you come along and decide that (a) this cute little fellow must have lost his mother and (b) a baby wolverine is just what you've always wanted in your apartment, anyway.

Remind yourself that a wild pet is not merely a weekend visitor. If he lives long enough, he will be your responsibility 365 days and nights a year. You may have to change his bedding in the rain or in freezing cold. And there he is, needing to be fed while you take your summer vacation. His appetite can cause problems too: he may have started on nice, handy warm milk, but now he's got to have a mouse a day. And where are you going to get all those mice?

But suppose your new family member *was* a genuine orphan. Suppose you have discovered a diet more easily obtained than mice: canned dog food and cod liver oil, for instance. Further, you are willing to give him daily care and even share his growing pains in spite of a nipped finger or two. What's to prevent you from giving it a try?

Nothing—if the law is willing. Every state and province of the United States and Canada has a whole shelf of regulations about wild animals. Better check your local laws before you welcome that wildling into your family circle. It may sound strange, but it's far easier to get a license to kill an animal than it is to keep one alive.

My wife, Peg, and I have a unique situation here on our old Vermont farm. With our nearest human neighbor a quarter-mile distant, and with no stray dogs or cats to worry about, our whole place has become a giant sanctuary. Not even a fence is necessary. The overgrown fields and meadows are bordered by a river in front and dense woodland on the sides. So some animal down on his luck can be released in the old hollow tree, say, or in the rock pile or briar patch, along with plenty of food. Chances are we'll see him around for days, sometimes weeks, until he's strong enough to go his own way.

Even creatures not protected by law—porcupines and crows, for instance—can go their own ways on our land with little help from us. Once an animal has learned that he is living in a freeloader's paradise, the problem is not so much to keep him as to get rid of him. A pair of orphaned chipmunks we raised in a fallen birdhouse came back for more than two years. They learned to push the screen door open and scamper across the kitchen floor to a dish of sunflower seeds in the corner. Having filled their cheek pouches, they'd scurry away without a backward glance. The whole

21

performance, needless to say, left a lasting impression on guests who stopped by for coffee.

Incidentally, professional pet dealers usually have permits to sell various native birds and animals. But better check local laws before you shell out for some contraband creature. It may be all right for the dealer to sell it, but not for you to buy it. Then, too, there are states and provinces where a valid bill of sale from the dealer makes everything legal, even though a native-born specimen from your own backwoods would be taboo.

Don't forget that, even if your star boarder remains friendly and inexpensive and legitimate, the day is bound to come when you wish to return him to the wild. The process is not as easy as it seems. The one peril that your pet has never faced is that of competition. When you drive out to the country on a Sunday afternoon to "give him his freedom," he finds the whole world arrayed against him. His own brethren will have nothing to do with him; they have their individual territories and he becomes the intruder wherever he goes. He is Odd Man Out.

Bewildered, he finds nowhere to turn. His daily peanut butter sandwich is no longer in a dish six inches from his nose. A hawk swoops at him, a dog chases him. Humans, once his benefactors, no longer reach down to cuddle him, but regard his advances with suspicion. His senses dulled by captivity, he is marked for failure.

You can help him if you remember that a wild animal is just that: a wild animal. Peanut butter may be fine at first, when the big problem is to keep him alive. But peanut butter is a scarce commodity in the wild. Find out what he'd eat under normal conditions and feed him accordingly: fruit and greens, for example, if he's a vegetarian.

Or, if he's a meat eater and you are squeamish

22

about mice, help him get the idea with a few fresh roadside-killed frogs or other small animals. Add an occasional grub or earthworm for variety. Not exactly what he can expect in the wild, but a lot more natural than a plate of dog food.

As the time approaches for your pet's release, allow him a longer period away from his enclosure each day. Put his food where he can find it once he's made his getaway into the woods, and feed him in that same spot daily. Then, in case freedom is tougher than captivity, he can at least stock up occasionally at your larder.

If there are no fields and woods close by your back door, you'd better invite some lucky landowner along on your walks. Then, when the two of you discover an orphaned opossum or battered bird, your friend can have the responsibility right from the start. Otherwise, if you take that lonesome bird or animal home, you may discover there's a long, long string attached.

Here, admittedly, I have been dealing with the problem at its worst. There are plenty of potential pets that may work out just fine. A friend of mine found a turtle wandering on a superhighway seven years ago. He scooped her up in the face of oncoming traffic, brought her home, made a leafy nest for her in the bathroom closet, and she has been a family member ever since. Another friend is raising and photographing his latest generation of cecropia moths. They began with a batch of eggs that he found, glued like tiny clay pots, on the underside of a leaf three summers ago.

In our own home, Peg and I have had a pair of terrestrial hermit crabs, each living in its adopted snail shell the size of a golf ball, for more than two years. It's a conversation-stopper when I remove one of the crabs from my pocket, lay it casually on the table, and the "empty" shell starts to walk away.

So not always does Irresistible Pet mean Insoluble Problem. If so, this book would be mercifully short. Its whole text would consist of three words: Don't Do It. But, like anything that's worthwhile, there's plenty of give-and-take involved. With almost any pet the "give" and "take" will work both ways. And there, happily, is the pleasure of it all.

Granted, then, that you have utilized a bit of Horse Sense—that good native intelligence most of us express in our more lucid moments—and have adopted some creature suited to your own situation. Now for a few words of Common Sense, or the means whereby you can make your pet at home in his new surroundings. Then some remarks on T.L.C.—Tender Loving Care, without which nearly any living thing may be doomed to disaster.

Basically, a living creature has two needs: food and shelter. Involved in these needs are a place to breed and produce young, to sleep, to find food and eat it safely, and to escape from enemies. This whole complex of conditions is met in the wild by what is called the animal's habitat. A successful enclosure for your pet should include a bit of that habitat. It should be, for him, a miniature Slice of Life.

Suppose the new arrival is a frog. Fresh from science class, it accompanied your son home on the bus. It will get along well in a vivarium that combines both land and water, as frogs are amphibians and demand a bit of each. On the other hand, if the latest family member is a rodent it should be housed in a box of dry, nibbleproof material. A few rodents do not even need a water dish, because they get all necessary moisture from their food.

With reptiles, the critical factor may be warmth. Some snakes, for example, must have nearly as much heat as a nest of baby birds. But full, undiluted sunlight can be fatal. Even a tropical desert snake can expire of sunstroke. Sunshine, yes—but shade too.

My friend's ravenous cecropia caterpillars demand food constantly. To supply that demand, he makes a daily shuttle run to an old apple orchard. Bringing in a few sprigs of fresh leaves, he puts them beside the remains of the old ones. The caterpillars finish the meal they are working on (trimming every leaf down to the midrib) and then obligingly move over onto the new greenery and keep right on eating. They never stop until it's time to spin their cocoons. Then, having pupated, they remain in their silken sleeping bags for ten months—while everybody gets a much-needed rest.

With such variety among your potential boarders, it's important to be aware of an animal's normal living conditions and to approximate those conditions as closely as you can. Each creature has a quirk—actually, thousands of quirks—that make it unique in the animal kingdom. The frog, for example, is totally carnivorous—except for a stray twig or sand grain that gets stuffed into its mouth along with a hapless dragonfly. But its prey must be moving to attract the frog. The dragonfly was quite safe, within inches of that cavernous maw—until it moved.

In the same way, the piece of liver or beef you put in the vivarium for the frog must be moving too. You have to poke it and make it jiggle. Otherwise you end up with just what you started with—a chunk of meat and a hungry frog.

Some turtles must swallow their food under water. Others chew their victuals where they find them, even if it's a cactus flower in the desert. One bird gulps its food in chunks while another subsists largely on liquids.

There is as much variety among other living creatures, too. For instance, flying squirrels make wonderful pets, but they keep late hours. Their day's activities begin around dusk. So if you value your sleep, better leave the flying squirrels to someone on the night shift. Their pudgy cousins the woodchucks, on the other hand, retire at sundown for the night. And then they retire in October for the winter. So food and shelter become a matter of *where* and *when* as well as *what*.

There is also the matter of *how much*. A tarantula I once had would eat a piece of meat the size of a large marble in one sitting—but her version of a sitting lasted twenty-four hours. And there was more than a month between meals. At the other extreme is the baby bird whose food arrives every few minutes. That insistent, begging mouth may funnel down more than twice the bird's weight in the time between dawn and dusk. On a human scale, this translates to a hundred loaves of bread, half a dozen hams and a five-gallon jug of milk daily. So, if you plan to rescue a fledgling and do it right, better do it on a Friday night. Then you'll have the whole weekend to feed him a meal every quarter hour. That is, if you want to come even close to the treatment he'd get at home.

Birds and mammals need all that food for warmth as well as energy and growth. A bird in pinfeathers or a tiny pink mouse, groping blindly for food, can catch a chill in a minute. On the other hand, many reptiles, amphibians, fishes, insects and their kin, with no body heat to maintain, will make fewer demands on you as a foster parent. There is no hidden furnace to stoke. If the temperature drops, so does the creature's metabolism—the rate at which it lives.

I remember seeing, a few years ago, dramatic evidence of the effect of growing conditions on a batch of tadpoles. A fifth grader brought them to me in a container cradled carefully under his arm.

"These are all my friends," he announced, "but I

26

have to let them go. My mother won't let me keep them any more."

I dutifully scrutinized his "friends." They were wood frog tadpoles, about thirty of them, with bodies the size of the eraser on the end of a pencil. I could guess why the lad's mother wanted him to release them. The container was quite obviously the large bowl from her electric mixer. A number of rings around the inside, plus the dark complexion of the water, showed that it had been the tadpoles' home since their days as eggs. Besides, it emitted a decidedly swampy aroma. All it needed was mosquitoes.

Release point for the tads, I learned, was the same place he had found them—a small pond behind the school. So at his invitation I accompanied him to watch the captives swim to freedom. Around us trooped the whole fifth-grade class.

When we got there, I showed him how to get the tadpoles gradually used to the chill waters. Then, after we had turned them loose, one of his classmates made a discovery. "Here's some of the other ones, Jerry," he called. "Only these didn't grow. You can start all over again."

We looked at this latest find. The tads were less than half the size of their newly released brothers—not much bigger than the fragment that snaps off when you break a pencil lead. A few of them still clung to the flimsy jelly of the egg mass. The mass had been there, stuck to the same submerged tree branch, on the day Jerry had collected his own frog eggs. Held in check by cold days and chilly nights, these tads had lagged far behind those in Jerry's cozy kitchen. Although surrounded by plenty of the algae on which they thrive, they had developed far more slowly.

Thus warmth is important, even to those creatures we often call cold-blooded. Important, too, as Jerry's

27

mother would agree, is the type and size of the container. More on this subject follows in the chapters on the various animal groups, but here are a couple of points to consider with almost any animal.

First, the enclosure should match the enclosed. My friend's three dozen caterpillars need no cage at all. They spend their lives on the leafy twigs he brings and puts into a vase. To the caterpillars the leaf means food, water and even shelter. As long as new leaves keep arriving daily, why move?

More shelter is required for the baby bird tossed out of its nest by the wind. It needs a close-fitting home for warmth and to keep it from tumbling around. Keith Armstrong's pet clam spent its days in a ten-gallon aquarium. There were four inches of sand on the bottom so the clam could plow around to its heart's content—if clams, which, indeed, do have hearts, also experience contentment.

The twelve garter snakes I had as a preteen-ager lived several summers in a six-by-six-foot wire enclosure in our back yard. Actually this cage was far larger than necessary. The snakes spent most of their time basking in the sun or draped over each other like participants in an encounter group.

But Sparky, a gray squirrel who cast his lot with us for a summer, was different. He had an entire maple tree for his home. When we went walking he'd run along with us, dashing up one tree after another. In one memorable fit of playfulness he jumped on a cow's back and stampeded the whole herd just as they were about to enter the barn for milking. For Sparky, any cage would have been too small.

The second point about any prospective pet is to try to plan ahead. Here, again, use your common sense. Obviously, it's better to work out minor details like how you're going to keep your pet *before* you get it, rather than after. I recall one time trading two

white mice for a bantam rooster. I brought the rooster home in a burlap bag and set it down in the kitchen. Then, calling my mother and sister to watch, I opened the bag.

Out popped two pounds of indignant fowl with its feathers decidedly ruffled. Mother and Irma fled to the living room and slammed the door in its face. I retreated into the closet. The rooster, with the kitchen all to itself, flew up on top of the cabinet and crowed defiance to the entire world.

Slowly I emerged from the closet, holding a jacket as if it were a bullfighter's cape. We got the rooster back in his bag and Mother made me take him to Wheeler's place down the road. Mr. Wheeler allowed me to release the rooster among a flock of terror-stricken Rhode Island Red hens. The whole performance lasted scarcely half an hour, but it taught me the value of foresight. I recommend it to you, too. Then you'll not have to ask yourself, as I did in those unsettled moments behind the closet door, "What will I do now?"

Cages and pens and enclosures can be made of a number of materials, including chicken wire, screening or boards. Cages for small animals can be made of cake racks or old refrigerator shelves wired together to form sides, top and bottom. But make them strong enough. Once a creature has learned that a cage can be defeated, it will work twice as hard to get out of it again. If the animal digs or burrows, have the wire of the enclosure go well down below ground. If it hops or climbs or flies you'll need some kind of screening for the top of the enclosure.

While planning ahead, consider what you will do during the cold season. If your animal sleeps in winter, it is best to allow it to go its way and find a suitable location. If you keep it, you will have to be sure it has enough shelter. Hibernating animals go into near-death sleep, with only a few heartbeats per minute and respiration so slow that you usually cannot detect it. But such a creature can freeze as well as any other, so a good sleep area must be provided.

Our raccoons burrowed down among the hay bales in the barn, and two of our four skunks tunneled well below its stone foundation. A woodchuck who had the run of the place managed to make his way into the hatchway of the cellar. He gnawed through the inner door and buried himself in the soil of the earthen floor. Peg and I found him, about two weeks after Groundhog Day, sampling a box of apples in the corner. After he went back to sleep we repaired the door he had nibbled through. When he awoke in March he chewed his way out again—this time taking part of the casing as well.

You should be careful that the cage is not too cramped and confining. A good rule, which must take into account an animal's activity, is to make the cage at least twice the length and breadth and height of its stretched-out, relaxed inhabitant. It's better, if possible, to have no cage at all. And since it's normal for almost any living creature to exist without physical bonds or fetters, there is little likelihood that a cage can be too large. But the animal must learn to regard the cage as its home—or it must have some kind of place within the caged area as its own private domain.

At this point we come to the final part of our chapter—Tender Loving Care. An entire garage or a screened porch can serve in a pinch as an enclosure for a young chipmunk that you rescued from a cat, but only if it has some corner that is uniquely its own. There, in a cereal box or coffee can, nestled in bedding that has its familiar smell, the chipmunk can lick its wounds and start on the road to recovery.

But chipmunks live in family groups when young. Although your small charge will later become solitary, he needs companionship now. So, if one chipmunk is all you have, you will need to play the role of a fellow chipmunk. If you handle him, and move his bedding a bit the way his brothers and sisters might be expected to do, he may flourish. Neglected except for food and water, he may fail.

You can be a Big Brother at other times, too, without even being present. Sounds are important to animals. Dr. Donald Gill, a veterinarian friend, bought a radio to put in the convalescent ward of his hospital. He has never turned it off. It goes on and on, year after year. The inmates keep up on the latest news, weather and music and seldom become the yapping, tumultuous rabble usually found in such places. Not that I'd suggest you keep the Hi-Fi going for a lonesome chipmunk or for two ounces of deer mouse, but the sounds of life around him will keep an otherwise solitary animal from becoming too solitary for his own well-being.

One easy trick is to set a clock where its ticking is audible to your small guest. The clock's steady beat will provide companionship, while the vibration of its action may help substitute for slight movements of the creature's missing family.

A whole host of mysterious ills can strike a young animal overnight. Many of these ailments will never get started if the foundling's interest in life is kept high. One way to maintain interest is to provide warmth—nice, steady warmth. It is incredible what a difference a little warmth will make in an animal's outlook. Even in midsummer, if people report that their adoptee is listless, I suggest a heating pad. If no heating pad is available, a flannel-covered jar of warm water or even an electric light bulb will help.

Be sure there's some way for the youngster to escape the heat when he has had enough. You want to comfort him, not cook him. Although young animals huddle in the nest for warmth, they crawl away from each other when they need to cool off. It's a good idea to locate the heating pad—suitably waterproof and nibbleproof so you don't electrocute him —under only a portion of the animal's cage. Put his hot water jug in one corner so he can cuddle up to it if the mood strikes him. Focus the heat from the light bulb by means of a cone of aluminum foil. Then keep a watchful eye on your new arrival for the next few hours. You can judge his reaction by where he positions himself in the box.

So, with the little stranger warmed and fed and snoozing in his corner to the rhythm of the alarm clock, you can take a deep breath. One hurdle passed. There are many more to go, but you can take them as they come. At least for the present, Wee Willie is well and happy and living among the facial tissues in a shoe box.

Right now his wild personality is manifested only in moments of alertness, his jumping at a sudden sound, or the way he eats his food. Further happy revelations, like the quick flurry of temper, the flash of independence that sometimes seems like plain orneriness, will appear as fluff turns to feathers and fuzz to fur.

Then, at last, the decision you have been putting off for weeks must be made. Wee Willie has become Big Bill—in more ways than one. And so you turn to the game warden, the veterinarian, the scout leader, the biology teacher, or anybody who might be able to help.

But don't call me. Chances are my phone will be busy anyway.

3. Ten Pets on a Pinhead

Three years ago we were invited to a friend's graduation. He was to receive a Ph.D. in biology. The program listed each candidate for an advanced degree along with the topic of his doctoral thesis. We looked at the titles: "The Flügelspiel Reaction in an Election Year," "Z-Wave Studies on Alpha Centauri," and "Is the Brünnhilde Complex Applicable to the Twentieth Century?"

We scanned the list further for Phil's name. Twice during his studies we had visited him, and both times we found him peering through a microscope. I had asked him what he was working on, and his preoccupied reply was echoed now on the program before us. There it was, among all the other learned titles: "A Pint of Pond Water."

Phil had learned, as I have also discovered, that while great events occur in politics, astronomy and sociology, there is also an endless array of wonders in muddy water. In a way, his studies were as important as any of them. Ponds and swamps are basic links in the food chain that eventually stretches out onto the land. Indeed, it is thought that the first living thing may have stirred in some primeval pond or tide pool, creeping through the slime somewhat like the amoeba under Phil's watchful eye.

"I studied that pint of water for nearly two years," Phil recalled. "I analyzed it and kept track of its chemistry as different plants and animals flourished and died. I did everything but take its pulse as I worked out the complex web of life among its inhabitants. I got to know them so well that they became like so many pets."

That's what this chapter is about: "pets" so small you can put ten of them on a pinhead. But don't sell them short just because they are so tiny. These infinitesimal pets are big business. Every Christmas, and all through the year at birthday time, thousands of parents and assorted other relatives search the stores for just the right present for budding Pasteurs. And as a result thousands of lucky boys and girls receive a microscope gift kit—complete with tweezers, glass slides and instruction book.

Often, unfortunately, the tweezers and slides are of better quality than the microscope. High magnification is only half the story; being able to see clearly what is magnified is the other half. But kids are resourceful and imaginative, and just glimpsing shadowy, out-of-focus shapes darting around beneath their noses is well worth the bleary eyes that may accompany the performance.

Perhaps you yourself are among the young Pasteurs and Leeuwenhoeks. If so, these next few pages may help you better understand the display that springs to life beneath your lenses. And, in case the price of even a toy microscope is beyond the reach of your allowance—as it was beyond mine as a youngster—I've included plans for making your own instrument.

Perhaps we should start there—with that homemade microscope. One can be fashioned readily out of an old tin can. Yet, incredibly, its optical quality is as good as the 'scopes you find in the average gift set —indeed, often better than most. I made my first one when I was in the sixth grade. I made my latest one this morning, just to be sure I could still do it. It took slightly under five minutes.

All you need is a strip of tin about the length and general shape of the blade of a common table knife. Round off all edges so it can be held comfortably next to your eye. Half an inch from one end drill a tiny round hole the size of a pencil lead, about a sixteenth of an inch in diameter. Smooth the edges of the hole with fine sandpaper. Touch a drop of water to the hole with a toothpick and presto, there's your microscope!

What makes it work? Simple!—the water drop rounds itself into a powerful little lens. So efficient is this lens that it magnifies objects, with marvelous clarity, about a hundred times larger than life. You could easily pry into the private lives of Phil's pet protozoans with this primitive 'scope. You could analyze them, if you wished, nearly as well as he can with his expensive instrument.

As with most microscopes, the object seen has to be so thin or transparent that light will shine through it. This transparency makes the details of its structure visible. For my light source I put a fifteen-watt electric bulb in a cigar box. A quarter-inch hole in the box allows light to shine up through the center of a large sewing spool. A flat piece of glass on the spool holds the object to be viewed. You have to work at close quarters. Bend down until your microscope is poised a quarter-inch away from the object, and your eye is a quarter-inch above that. Now the reason for the spool becomes apparent: there's room for your nose. And there, hunched over, awkward but enchanted, you can peer at the tiny innards of a creature whose existence would be hidden from you except for a strip of tin and a drop of water.

Your small charges will be oblivious to that Eye from above. They will go about their lives as if still in their pond, taking in food, warding off enemies, respiring, reproducing. Indeed, these motes of life carry on all the basic functions that we do.

Such detail is remarkable when you realize that the common amoeba is smaller than a grain of salt. Then consider that the amoeba feeds on even smaller protozoans—which, in turn, consume bacteria by the thousands. An entire world in a waterdrop!

You'll see all sorts of strange antics—at least they are strange to our way of thinking. You'll discover creatures that crawl, or leap, or stretch-hump-and-stretch like a measuring worm. You'll find villains and victims. One villain—the didinium—cruises through the water with a clockwise spin, looking like a tiny baseball. When it bumps against a victim—paramecium—it plunges a sucking tube into the hapless creature. And once it has reduced the slipper-shaped paramecium to the general contour of an old sock, it disengages and goes spinning away in search of its next victim.

Another activity that always excites interest is that of reproduction. The common amoeba splits in two; thus it multiplies by dividing, so to speak. Certain forms of paramecium join together in a sort of mating. But it's not really sex as it is known in the higher forms of animals, since there are neither male nor female paramecia. It's apparently a matter of exchanging material from the nucleus of each individual—a sort of mutual rejuvenation. Then, at a future date, each paramecium sedately splits in two.

Your miniature metropolis may also present you with one of the most puzzling bits of life in the micro-world: volvox, the revolutionary. Volvox is closely related to tiny beings whose internal workings are laced with small capsules containing chlorophyll, the familiar green stuff of plants. So the group to which it belongs is sometimes called the plant-like animals—and at other times, sensibly enough, the animal-like plants. Members of the group may be claimed by botanists on Tuesdays and Thursdays, and by zoologists on Mondays, Wednesdays and Fridays.

This is not all that's puzzling. There's doubt as to whether volvox is an "it" or a "them." The body is composed of many cells, rather than just one. The cells are arranged in a layer to form a hollow sphere. This sphere rolls along like a miniature bowling ball, or like the earth in an eccentric orbit. Within it may be a smaller volvox, known, perhaps with a glint of satisfaction by the botanists, as a bud. The bud gets larger until finally its "parent" bursts and it is "born." Pregnant plant or pregnant protozoan; either way it's interesting to ponder.

You may find other creatures of your own to equal or exceed any that you meet in these pages. But, like any other living things, they all have certain requirements for their livelihood. They must have the right conditions of moisture, temperature and habitat. The small organisms already mentioned live in water, but your miniature zoo can be scraped from the moist, green bark at the base of a tree or it can be lifted intact from a mossy patch in a shady glen. There, existing in the film of moisture, you will find creeping, crawling, swimming creatures by the hundreds—even thousands.

But ponds dry up. The sun shifts through the year

and turns a cool glen into a miniature desert. The inhabitants die by the millions. But more millions escape. They develop a hard membrane around themselves, impervious to sun or heat. Within this membrane a few molecules of water and protein and other substances lie in the dust and wait—sometimes for years—until the welcome moisture comes again.

Lifted by air currents, tossed by winds, these cysts become wanderers in little space capsules. Some crash into the icy slopes of Mt. Everest. Others come to rest on the scorching sands of the Sahara. But countless others settle in fields and meadows and forests—a silent, unseen rain of life, drifting down, night and day.

You can collect a few of these pioneers and bring them back, as it were, from the dead. Take a small handful of dry grass or hay and put it in a jar of water. Rainwater is best, as it contains no chlorine or harmful chemicals from water pipes. If you must use tap water, boil it five minutes and set it out in the open for two days to neutralize itself.

Place your infusion, as it is called, in a spot well lighted but not in direct sunshine. Keep it uncovered and at room temperature. After a few days the water will become cloudy. This cloudy water, under your microscope, will be seen to consist of swarms of minute objects just within the limits of visibility. These minute objects are bacteria.

Then, sometime around the fifth day, the swarm is pushed aside as you watch, like a crowd parting before a dignitary's automobile. Into your field of view comes The Notable—a paramecium, perhaps, or one of fifty thousand other protozoan varieties. It looks gigantic compared to its bacterial neighbors as it scoops them up by the thousands in its funnel-shaped, never-closing mouth.

You have given new life to a protozoan after its great sleep—or short sleep, depending on how long it had been adrift before it settled on your wisp of grass. That sedately cruising animalcule may have left the shores of Lake Superior ten years ago, or it may have been dusted into the air from McGinty's Swamp just last week.

Now that your small pet is back in circulation, it goes about doing what any pet might do: producing more of its kind. Under the microscope, you will observe that it develops a wasp waist, as if an invisible belt were tightening around its middle. The "waist" gets slimmer until, in an hour or so, your single organism becomes two, traveling along in tandem. The two organisms break apart, grow for a few hours, and divide again.

By the next day there is a sprinkling of protozoans. They slice through the hordes of bacteria, eating and growing and reproducing. A population explosion is in the making. It feeds itself on the bacterial population explosion. And the prime mover for it all is the food released by the decay of those pieces of grass in the water.

This is only the beginning of the parade. Your protozoans double their numbers every few hours until the water is so thick with them that they bump into each other. Now they gather near the surface, for here the oxygen is richer. If such small creatures could be said to experience distress, it must be setting in now.

Now comes the next unit in the parade. Perhaps it is didinium, that prowler with the soda-straw mouthpiece. Or it may be stentor, whose funnel-shaped body seems to be all mouth as it takes in bacteria or fellow protozoans with happy impartiality.

And so on. You can watch each variety flourish and fade, depending on the food supply—and, of course, on what dried specimens were on those wisps of grass in the first place. Charge the batteries, so to speak, with a few more pieces of grass (or hay) every week and your tempest in a teapot will go on forever.

Most of the early animals in your infusion will be single-celled organisms—or noncellular, as many scientists prefer to call these complex protozoans. Gradually, however, you begin to note one small individual that, for lack of a better description, can be likened to a portly ballerina with a wheel on her head.

This improbable being is a rotifer, whose pointed "slippers" are really a two-toed foot to anchor it in place. From the foot, this protozoan expands into a barrel-shaped body (the "ballerina" is well past her prime) tapering off with one or two "wheels." These so-called wheels are actually bands of hairlike cilia rotating in succession, sucking food down into a capacious gullet.

The internal workings may remind you of one of those transparent models of people or dogs or horses—except that these innards are in motion. There are two chomping jaws halfway down the throat. There is a small but impressive stomach, an ovary with eggs (unless it is one of the rare males that seem to be in the process of phasing out in the evolution of the group), and even a tiny anus to get rid of the many products of this activity. And all this contained within a body no larger than the period at the end of this sentence. Small wonder that my friend said his pint of water was too big—he should have studied a spoonful!

And, speaking of that pint of water, your pet parade is increased enormously when your source is a handful of gunk from the bottom of a nearby pond or swamp. Now you will find members of many of the groups that make up our more familiar world—the worms, molluscs, insects and their relatives. You'll see crustaceans, too—cyclops, for instance, named after the one-eyed monster of mythology. It looks somewhat like a sandgrain-sized lobster, with a central ruby-red eye and long feathery antennae that propel it jerkily through the water. Its cousin, daphnia, about the same size, is a favorite tropical fish food; we'll meet it again in the fish chapter.

As you watch, one of these lilliputian cousins of the crab may blunder into a diminutive "tree" whose "limbs," an eighth of an inch long, wrap around its victim in a paralyzing embrace. This miniature terror is the hydra, named after the mythical sea serpent with nine heads. The hydra's paralyzing sting cells quiet its prey, which is then engulfed by a mouth within the center of those tentacles.

Its prey is sometimes larger than the hydra itself, whose jellylike body stretches heroically to encompass it. Now the hydra looks a bit odd, with tentacles stretched from its bulging body—like a small boy reaching for more food while his mouth is already stuffed.

The hydra and its prey form just one small segment of this watery world. Every drop will tell its own story. And you can pack still more drama into a drop by concentrating your catch. This can be done simply by pouring pond or swamp water through fine-mesh cloth, such as a nylon stocking. Swimming and floating organisms, known as plankton, will remain on the cloth. Then, when you wash them off into a little water, you have a thin soup of vibrant life. Keep this soup refrigerated when not in use and it will last for days.

Not all the inhabitants of your pint of pond water will belong to the animal world. You will see exquisite, fragile-appearing spheres, crescents, rods—even diminutive doughnuts. Green, red or brown, these jewels are diatoms, desmids and other algae. One common canoe-shaped form cruises slowly through the water by some ghostly locomotion still not clearly understood. Here you meet the animal-like plants (or plant-like animals) again. Often they are lumped with the

42

protozoans in a single third kingdom, the protists, as set apart from the plant and animal kingdoms.

It is impossible to guess what types of creatures, from protists to polliwogs, may be found in your micro-menagerie. To be able to enjoy them as long as possible, keep them on the cool side, out of direct sunlight. Those tiny algae will convert wastes and carbon dioxide to food and oxygen, but their concentration is probably not great enough to supply all the needs of their neighbors. So keep your contained community in a shallow bowl with plenty of surface area for air absorption. Add rainwater or pond water to compensate for evaporation. It's also a good idea to add a bit of dried plant material or a grain of boiled wheat weekly.

Biologists feel there may be as many more creatures undiscovered, even in our enlightened age, as there are now known to science. So, there is a chance that among your "pets" will be an Unknown, new to you and to everyone else. Perhaps, if it is duly contemplated and catalogued, it may even be named after you.

There's a sequel to the tale of my college friend, by the way. I asked him what he did with that much-scrutinized pint of water when he was through with it.

"Oh," he said. "By that time I practically knew the shoe size and blood type of every one of the inhabitants. They were old friends, so I just couldn't toss them out. In fact, I didn't even want to abandon them in one of the college aquariums."

He grinned sheepishly. "Well, graduation weekend was nice weather, anyway. So my girl and I piled into a car—with our 'family' between us—and drove eighteen miles out into the country. Then I let them go, right where I'd found them two years before."

43

4. Snails Pace—or Do They?

There it is, in a small hand held out for your inspection. At first it looks like a wad of chewing gum, or a curled-up shoelace. But as you watch, the "shoelace" untangles itself. It stretches out as if pulled by some invisible hand, and starts off in your direction.

You are in the presence of any of several thousand assorted beings known to scientists as invertebrates because of their singular spinelessness. Whereas we —and our relatives the fishes, frogs, reptiles, birds and mammals—have a segmented backbone to keep us reasonably in shape, most invertebrates have no such refinement. They must shore themselves up by other means.

Soft-bodied snails develop a shell that they back-pack for life. Their less well-endowed cousins, the slugs, merely wear a thickened patch of tissue like a saddle, and keep their shape by body tension, some-what like an airfilled balloon. Insects and crustaceans are living suits of armor, pulled around by muscles from within.

Then there are the worms. These lissome bits of life come in many shapes and forms. They range from tiny microscopic threads to the impressive six-footers of the tropics. A few of them build tubes or cases of sand and other debris, but most of them merely hide for protection. They can change their body shape by muscular movements—to the fascination of fishermen, small boys and horrified little girls.

Any of these intriguing creatures may be bought to you in great high spirits by some young member of the family—and abandoned with equal gusto the follow-ing day. And there you are, staring at it apprehen-sively, wondering what to do next.

In many cases your unscheduled visitor is quietly consigned to the back yard, or the local pond, or the city park, in hopes that it will make its own way from there. But if the fate of a science project hangs in the balance, or if the Whatzit has captured your imagi-nation, you may wish to know how to proceed.

Actually the problem may not be as great as it seems. Just remember the two basic requirements of living things: food and shelter. In most cases food can wait, at least for awhile, so all you need to provide at the moment is shelter.

Generally the softer an animal the more it needs moisture. Hides and hair and tough skin cut down on evaporation, but such niceties are denied a naked slug on a piece of wood, or an earthworm out for a stretch after a rain. If such a creature should stray too far from shelter, it will dry up. A twisted trail of hardened slime on a sidewalk will tell its own story if you follow the trail to its end—a shriveled slug or a withered worm.

Snails can get around better than their less-protected cousins. Their shell gives them a big advantage against drying or bodily harm. If things outside get too harsh the snail can usually retreat until better times come along. Once I bought half a dozen edible snails at a specialty market and put them in a terrarium. They were dry looking and drawn far into their shells, but five of them were crawling around in an hour. The sixth, however, bided its time for more than two days. Probably it was playing possum; thus it might be overlooked. After all, an edible snail can get too much attention.

After you have scooped the last spoonful of mayonnaise or eaten the final pickle from a wide-mouthed gallon jar, you can fashion the jar into a small animal vivarium. By punching holes in the lid of such a container and then partially covering them you can control the moisture from soggy wet to bone dry.

Lay the large jar on its side. Secure its neck to a block of wood scooped out to receive it; this will tilt the jar a bit from the horizontal and steady it so it cannot roll and create an unscheduled earthquake. Remember to keep the container well away from radiators and direct sunlight—unless your pets happen to be those rare creatures that live in hot springs. It's better to have things a bit cool—around 65°F.—than to have a one-gallon sauna in the making.

In setting up this vivarium, place a layer of small pebbles in the bottom. It won't matter if you spill a little water now and then; the surplus will merely drain down among the stones. Next, add a layer of coarse sand or gravel. Nestle a small jar-lid in the sand to serve as a tiny pool. Arrange things so the rim of the pool will be flush with the final level of the soil. The pool should be where you can reach it easily in case one of your tenants turns out to be less of a swimmer than you thought.

When you obtain a potential resident for your vivarium, find out, if you can, what surroundings the animal was in when it was captured. Was it under a rock? Poking along on an old log? Burrowing in sand? Bulldozing through the mud? How about plants, trees —what kind were growing there? Important facts, these, when you consider that the creature was probably doing fine until somebody came along and spoiled things.

Now it's up to you to make everything all right again. Duplicate the native habitat as closely as you can: stones, plants and a seedling tree or two. The roots of even the smallest trees affect the chemistry of the soil.

You will want some of that native earth, too. Take home an extra supply while you're about it. Then you can replace soil that might become fouled while you're learning. Or, in case your enthusiasm runs away with you, you could eventually graduate your pets from their jug to a posh ten-gallon condominium and they'd still tread familiar soil.

Introduce the topsoil to your pickle-jar vivarium, complete with rocks, bits of wood and other scenery. If some of the creatures need hiding places, tip the rocks up slightly.

Now for the landscaping. A bit of moss holds moisture well and creates a good resting place for animals. Poke holes in the soil and plug in the majority of the plants. You might save out a plant or two; you'll probably change your mind about the arrangement after the creatures have wandered around, and this means you'll need a little spare greenery.

As long as you're creating your own little countryside, use your imagination. Insert a scraggly twig for variety; it will be explored by snails and insects and serve as a framework for spider webs. A barberry twig with fruit will add a splash of color; or use a sprig of holly, black alder or partridge berry—they all bear scarlet fruit. Red osier and willow have red and yellow twigs, respectively, and can be used to good effect.

Doubtless you'll want to use your vivarium for more than one kind of creature, and some of them may jump up or leap or otherwise scramble to get away. And the jagged edges of nail holes in the cover of the vivarium are hardly the most hospitable of surfaces. So when you make the holes in the metal lid of the jar for ventilation, be sure to drive the nail in from the underside out. Then frantic, or even curious animals cannot hurt themselves. Place a sheet of transparent food wrapping over part of the cover to control the amount of moisture. This technique works equally well if the mouth of the jar is covered with a screen or cloth, rather than with the metal lid.

If possible, leave your vivarium uninhabited for two or three days. This will allow the plants to take root before some enthusiastic denizen can upheave them. A few days' grace will also let you see how moisture conditions will be. If the sides of the glass are dripping wet, you need fewer plants, a less generous swim pool, or more ventilation.

Only you know what animals will go into your zoo-in-a-bottle. Some will be discussed here, and others in later chapters. But when you do put animals in the vivarium, it's a good idea to have them all about the same size. Otherwise, if you put three small creatures in with a large one, you may find that you end up with one single gigantic creature and no little ones. There's not much banding together for protection in this corner of the animal kingdom.

To prevent one animal from making a meal of its neighbor, be sure there's a good food supply. Chances are you'll have some creatures that eat only plants, others that capture living prey, and still others that are not fussy in either direction. Your job is to figure which is which. Then you must provide for their respective needs before they take the task upon themselves.

Among the more fearsome of your small charges will be spiders, certain beetles, and centipedes. The appetites of these creatures can be assuaged with a piece of cooked egg, or a bit of hamburger and a few lately expired flies. Spiders, as a rule, will eat only if they can catch their own food, so a few active morsels are needed on their bill of fare.

Spiders and centipedes subdue their prey with poison fangs. It's impressive to see how fast those twin hypodermics can "make an insect think he's asleep," as one small naturalist described it.

There's little worry about nipped fingers, by the way. Common woods centipedes are harmless to humans. So are most of the spiders you'll find in open meadows and fields. The large garden spider, for example, looks quite imposing with its yellow and black clown suit and spectacular web. However, it has no designs on you in spite of its tigerlike coloration. But since this variety would need the whole jar to itself, you'd better stick to smaller specimens. There are hairy-brown wolf spiders, for instance, or the pepper-and-salt-colored jumping spiders that may remind you of tiny bulldogs as they squat on the lookout for a passing insect. Even if any of these spiders should bite, you'd scarcely notice it—or else think it was a mosquito.

Both the poisonous black widow and brown recluse spiders are shy and found in dark places. The female black widow is pea-sized, shiny black, usually with a red or orange hourglass marking on the underside of her abdomen. The brown recluse is also small, with the pattern of a violin on its back, giving it the name of "fiddleback spider." Chances are you'll never see either one, but such is their reputation (although there have been only a few dozen proven fatalities in all of American medical history) that they should be mentioned here.

The more sedate plant eaters will subsist on native greenery, with an added fillip of lettuce or spinach leaf twice a week. Such a menu will do for most snails and slugs. Some plant-eating beetles will feed on any available foliage, while others will starve in what seems like the middle of plenty. Cucumber beetles, for instance, will systematically riddle the leaves of cukes and related species such as squashes and melons, but they turn up their noses at most other garden crops. On the other hand, you can feed a Japanese beetle on nearly three hundred separate plants—including poison ivy, if you don't mind possible consequences. Consequences, that is, to you and not the beetle, which takes the pesky vine in stride.

A word here about another creature that will eat almost anything: the lowly earthworm. This is a fascinating animal despite its seeming lack of personality. Its mental capacity, while admittedly limited, has been said to be about halfway between the know-nothing protozoans and know-it-all man. An earthworm can be taught to run a simple maze, such as choosing the right path (leading to cool, rewarding dampness) over the wrong one (ending in hot, dry sand). It can size up a potential bit of food and maneuver it so that it will best fit into the burrow. Thus it may explore a dead leaf until it locates the stem; then, grasping this "handle" with its prehensile upper lip, it successfully hauls it underground. Sometimes you can see a leaf curled halfway down into a burrow, where it had proved too large for the industrious worm to handle.

Earthworms often creep through the soil by surrounding it. They eat their way steadily forward, taking in sand grains, plant fragments and smaller organisms with total impartiality. In due time the worm voids the mass—minus many of the plant fragments and small organisms, but rich with waste materials. This mass, when voided aboveground, is known as the worm's casting. Castings are a welcome sight to the gardener who knows the value of this soil conditioner, but they are viewed less joyfully by the golfer who might miss a putt by virtue of this little pat of fertilizer.

Worms will make themselves at home in your vivarium soil, where they will burrow for bits of organic material. A few of yesterday's tea leaves and a pinch of this morning's coffee grounds will be accepted, as will crumbled hard-boiled egg yolk or powdered milk. But be careful not to turn your vivarium into a garbage heap. There should be no more food provided than is eaten in a given feeding period—which, for the nocturnal earthworm, is overnight.

You can keep earthworms in a wooden box of rich, moist soil with lawn clippings, or other plant material on top. Many youngsters have eased the strain on their family's fish-bait budget with their own earthworm farms. Superior varieties of worms with just the right wiggle to attract fishermen—and, hopefully, the fish—can be purchased from supply houses. But equally creditable livestock for the earthworm farm can be obtained at night on a lawn after a rain. A flashlight will be needed to find the worm, but you'll have to pounce fast. In spite of a total lack of eyes, the earthworm is somehow sensitive to light. It can snap back into its hole like a rubber band and all you will get is a handful of grass.

Incidentally, earthworms make excellent food for

other animals. If some small creature is indifferent to its daily fare, try snipping a bit of the tail section from an earthworm. The detached fragment will immediately be seized by an astonishing fit of convulsions, twisting and tossing enough to draw wide-eyed interest from almost any creature.

Although the loss of a part of its anatomy is unfortunate, the durable earthworm is equal to the occasion. It quickly escapes while its unfortunate nether section is abandoned to its fate. And everything works out all right, since the abbreviated worm soon grows a new posterior.

One final thought on the adaptability of earthworms —and, indeed, the flexibility of many living things, without which life in a bottle probably could not work. Although earthworms must have moisture and quickly die of exposure on a sunbaked sidewalk, they do have an additional method of protection. If drought parches the land, or if you let your vivarium dry out, the earthworms rise—or descend—to the occasion. Gathering by some signal, they cling to each other in a tight-knit ball. Thus they conserve life-giving moisture until the blessed rains come, or until you arrive with your watering can.

I once had a marsh-habitat vivarium that went from a swamp to a desert in the space of five weeks. I had been away on a trip, leaving directions for the care of all my pets, but forgetting to mention the vivarium on top of my filing cabinet. When I returned the vegetation was crisp and brown—almost as crisp as the dead salamander in the middle of the nonexistent pool.

I poked through the dusty remains. Yes, there they were, conserving the last iota of moisture—two earthworms, bundling together, in a corner beneath a patch of moss. They stretched and wriggled, as if grateful for new life when I laid them on a moistened spot in my window garden.

The powdery soil, crunchy plants and crumbly moss were consigned to the compost heap. The dish that had held the unfortunate salamander found its way to the back of my desk—dried mud and all. As a naturalist, I did not mind its crusted interior in the least, but began to use the dish as a repository for thumb tacks, rubber bands and assorted gadgetry.

The summer and winter passed. Another summer arrived, and one day a driving thunderstorm blew in and ruined everything on my desk.

Everything, that is, but three pond snails. Unnoticed in the thick caked mud, they had clung to the smooth surface of the dish for eight months, glued tightly by a film of dried mucus. Now, rejuvenated by the rain, they were in their glory—poking around in the mud and the paper clips.

I remember, too, when one of my terrestrial hermit crabs got off on the wrong track. It was sent to me, tongue in cheek, by a friend in Chincoteague, Virginia, one of the jolliest people I know. I had jokingly referred to him as crabby in a book I had written about horses, and we promptly named the creature Warren after its benefactor. I fed Warren bits of coconut, and often carried him around in my pocket, taking him out on any provocation, much to the delight of small bystanders and the dismay of their elders. He would run over eager hands and climb up willing sleeves. Then he would perch on a convenient shoulder and wave his antennae while he surveyed the world with myopic eyes on movable stalks.

One day I was an overnight guest at a friend's home. Usually I put Warren in a small pasteboard box upon retiring, but this time I forgot and left him in my shirt pocket. The next morning he was missing.

Sorrowfully, we went on our way. My companion

of nearly a year had to be somewhere in that rambling house, poking into a dusty corner or climbing up a window drape. But surely he'd die of thirst—if he didn't starve in the meantime.

I asked my friend to scatter crumbs of cornmeal and coconut along the baseboards, plus three or four jar lids filled with water. I returned home and weeks passed with no news of Warren. Then one day a little parcel arrived containing a few pathetic legs and a couple of body fragments.

The accompanying note said that this was all that was left of our protégé after the cat had finished with him.

Bereft, I ceased working on a story I had started about the personable little crustacean. Then I almost forgot about him, until the telephone rang more than a month later.

"Guess what!" said Andrew Gill, on the other end of the phone.

I guessed. But I let him tell me. And I was right; Warren had been found. After more than two months' wandering, he'd turned up in a bureau drawer. They'd heard him rustling around one evening when there was nothing on television. He had survived a full month after they'd quit putting out the food and water. There had been no further hope, they figured; hadn't they taken his remains away from the cat?

The "remains," of course, were merely the shed body covering of our missing pet. Not only had he survived; he had actually flourished. Casting off the unyielding outer skin, he'd moulted and grown bigger.

The old snail shell in which he'd been living was too tight, but it was all he had. Now it clung to his rear section like a caboose, scarcely covering that tender posterior.

Andrew mercifully gave him another home—a Florida snail shell about the size of a lemon. It was

somewhat large, but Warren quickly transferred to it, nevertheless. He dragged it manfully around for another six months until the cat struck again—this time for keeps.

That's the way with these so-called lesser animals, the invertebrates. They balance on the brink of disaster most of their lives. But give them a handful of soil, a little water and something to eat, and their antics will surprise you.

Undaunted, therefore, when some disconcerting creature comes to call, you can welcome it, if not with open arms, at least with an open mind—and a waiting vivarium.

Then just sit back and see what you can learn as you watch the snails pace.

5. Termites, Anyone?

My first experience in raising insects was when I was about ten years old. The lucky subjects were ten or a dozen clothes moths. And it all took place without being planned.

It seems that clothes moths feed on other foods besides wool sweaters, fur coats and an occasional pair of mittens. They have a taste for anything in the animal protein line—in my case, the carefully prepared skin of a Baltimore oriole that I found dead along the road.

I first knew something was wrong when the oriole began to moult. This, of course, is something a deceased bird is not supposed to do. It lay there, suitably plumped out with cotton, in the top bureau drawer; my first attempt at taxidermy. But when I picked it up to show to one of my chums, about a quarter of the feathers stayed behind.

Surprised, we inspected the oriole. More feathers fluttered to the floor. And before I was able to place the skin gingerly back in the drawer it had lost nearly half its plumage. That delicate membrane, so carefully dissected away from the bird's body several months before, was riddled with holes. Its cotton stuffing showed through in so many places that it looked as if the bird had been hit by a charge of buckshot.

We searched for the culprits. There was nothing to see but a dusting of gray, powdery material. Then, on looking in the drawer among those abandoned feathers, we discovered several tiny white cocoons, each the size of a small grain of rice. As I poked further, a few half-inch long insects flew out past our faces.

Clothes moths! I had never seen any before but I knew them by reputation. Don Brown and I chased them, squashing each one in righteous wrath. But, of course, the damage had been done. My oriole was ruined. And the powdery debris—"frass," or the undigested residue from feeding activity—lay there in the drawer for weeks until I decided it had taunted me long enough and threw the whole mess out.

I've raised thousands of insects since that time and, doubtless, have given a boost to thousands more as I unwittingly provided the springboard from which new generations could be launched. Every time a mosquito, for example, takes a good bite, the stage is set for a new crop of pesky insects. Many mosquitoes, it seems, must have a blood meal before they can produce hatchable eggs. And the small birds and animals we have encouraged around the place have left their imprint on the local lice and flea populations.

But there are many insects that are both harmless and useful. And fascinating as well. In helping them set up housekeeping, you will find as much enjoyment as the tropical fish hobbyist or the proud foster parent of a new litter of hamsters.

Like many of the animals in this book, a number of insects may be thrust on you whether you wish it or not. Most of the time you just open a window and shoo them out, but with a little care you can provide yourself with hours of entertainment. Within that Tinkertoy body you will discover a being who is as efficient in its way as you are.

If you have ever bent down to watch a praying mantis, for instance, and have had the creature turn its head and give you a solemnly searching look, you may know something about the personality packed within those little automatons.

If you'd like to try your hand at raising a few of these creatures, you can use the vivarium described in the last chapter. Or you can raise them in any properly furnished convenient container of the right size. Some insects, like the praying mantis, can be given the run of the house. However, such freedom can be a bit unsettling if the insect makes a crash landing on the shoulder of a guest who hasn't been briefed beforehand.

Since the mantis is one of the insects most frequently captured, it may be well to begin with this species. Many points regarding its care apply equally to others.

The praying mantis comes in various sizes, depending on species and sex. The female is larger than the male, and sometimes expresses her liberated nature by eating the male after mating. A lady Carolina mantis is impressive indeed, sometimes as much as four inches long, with a matronly rear section as large as your thumb.

In spite of its southern name, the Carolina mantis may be found as far north as Quebec or Michigan. Like a number of other creatures—the cardinal, mockingbird, and opossum, to name a few—it has been noted further north with each passing year. This may be due to an apparent warming trend in our climate.

As a boy I never met a mantis as far north as my home in Connecticut. The first one I saw was a belligerent specimen which stood its ground in the center of a street in New Rochelle, New York, and precipitated a traffic jam. Few people in New Rochelle had ever seen such an insect, either.

You can find mantis egg cases, looking like hardened masses of buffy styrofoam, on old weeds and even on the sides of buildings. They are half the size of an English walnut. Children often find them after the leaves are gone in the fall. If this should happen, it's best to allow them to remain in the cold until spring. The mantis nymphs will be ravenous on hatching, and if you have brought an egg case into a warm room prematurely, you'll find yourself with two or three hundred baby mantids in a few weeks—and without a fly or aphid in sight. And since mantids have no compunction about consuming their brothers, you'd very likely end up with one battle-scarred veteran—all by himself and still hungry.

There's another good reason for leaving any insect egg case or cocoon outside under normal weather conditions. If it stays out in the open it will get normal amounts of sunshine and rain. So if you should decide to bring it in, be sure to give it a little sprinkling of "rain" once or twice weekly. Many insects need moisture to enable them to break out of the egg or to fight their way free of the confines of a cocoon. An additional reason for leaving the egg case undisturbed is that the insect may not hatch if it hasn't gone through a long period of freezing weather to "age" its slumbering tissues.

On the other hand, it may be a bit hazardous for your potential insect guest to remain on a handy porch railing or windowsill until spring. Birds are quick to open a cocoon or crack through the tough exterior of an egg case—which, of course, is normal, since insects are natural food for birds. Then, too, mice will sometimes nip into them for the nourishment, and even cats and squirrels are not above eating a slumbering insect now and then.

There is one spot where overwintering insects will be safe: your refrigerator. But your family may have its own opinions as to the kind of eggs that should normally be found in the icebox. So place next spring's potential hatch in a pasteboard box with holes punched in its cover for air.

Cover the bottom of the box with a mattress of crumpled paper toweling; this will be a handy sponge for the weekly sprinkle of "rain" that still needs to be provided. It will also serve as a shock absorber to prevent injury to your charges. They are living creatures, in spite of their unyielding, inert appearance.

If you allow the mantis egg case to hatch under normal conditions, it should present you with several score of lively youngsters in mid-spring. They start to wander away after hatching, so keep an eye on the case, beginning in late April. Half a dozen of the hatchlings will be all you'll need in your vivarium. The rest can be scattered in your back yard or a nearby park, where they will give a few thousand plant pests their comeuppance.

Food for the hungry nymphs can be provided by a piece of ripe banana. Not that mantids have vegetarian tendencies; it's just that common fruit flies are attracted by the smell of banana. And mantids will eat fruit flies.

Place the banana right in the vivarium, if the holes in its cover are large enough to admit the sixteenth-of-an-inch flies. Or put it out in the open until it has gathered some of the little flies, and then transfer it to the vivarium. The flies will have laid eggs in the banana and thus will provide a continuous source of living food.

But suppose your attempt to gather fruit flies should fail, and your mantids are holding those predatory forelimbs jackknifed in "prayer" for the food that does not come. You can still save the day. A few minutes in a weedy patch of yard should produce several twigs covered with newly hatched aphids. Or you can collect small insects on the outside of a lighted windowpane after dark. To do this, invert a wide-mouthed jar over the insect, then slip a square of cardboard between jar and windowpane—and there's food for your mantids.

You can then release the insect into another jar by putting the two jar mouths together and slipping the cardboard out from between them. Point the bottom of one jar toward a strong light so that the insects will be drawn into it. Then you can go back to the windowpane and collect more insects. When you have enough, put the jar in the vivarium and slip off the cardboard cover. The captive insects will escape—from the frying pan into the fire.

As the young mantids get older they will grow by shedding their skins. You can watch the process of moulting as the old covering bursts and the tender new creature carefully pulls its body parts—legs, wing buds, even the slender antennae—out of its discarded shell.

Quickly the callow mantis pumps air into its still soft, fragile body—in effect blowing itself up like a balloon. After you have seen the completed task, you will think it was impossible for so large a creature to have fitted inside that shriveled skin. But after the insect has hardened a few hours, you will find that it is the same alert praying—or preying—mantis as before, only a third larger.

For the mutual safety of these fierce little creatures, put each mantis in a separate cage or compartment. Or, better still, when you have got the hang of how to care for them, let all of them go except the one or two you wish to keep. You do not need a complete vivarium for each one, but each should have its own twig and room enough to climb around in.

A little dew should be supplied daily in the form of sprinkled water. Supposedly the body fluids of its prey supply enough moisture, but if the mantis should happen to consume a dry fly it will readily accept a little extra liquid. Thrusting its pointed pixie chin deep into a droplet, the mantis drinks in a long, steady draught. Or sometimes you may see it licking flecks of moisture from its own body. It goes over every portion like a cat, carefully laving the steel-trap forelegs and pulling the fragile antennae slowly through its mouth, gently polishing them between lethal jaws.

Mating may take place under your watchful eye after you have put the sexes together, or it may be postponed indefinitely if the female mistakes her potential suitor's intentions and pounces on him. The confines of a vivarium scarcely give him a chance to escape. And even if a successful mating does take place, the female has been known to turn and systematically devour her partner. So, if you are bent on playing cupid, play it carefully. Feed the prospective bride well beforehand; the bridegroom, too, as he'll occasionally get the drop on his amazonian spouse.

Most of the time, however, mating is without incident. It has to be, or there'd be fewer mantids. The female lays her eggs a few days after mating has occurred. She deposits them in a bubbly mass that hardens on exposure to air. Slowly she moves up the tip of her abdomen back and forth as she gradually moves forward, building up that frothy egg case. Shortly after egg-laying, she loses her alertness and her interest in food. Then one morning, you will find her dead.

And so another mantis generation has completed its full circle. Put the egg case where birds or mice won't get it, keep it chilled through the winter, and 'round you go again.

Care of the praying mantis is much the same as the care of many other insects. If you begin with insect eggs, remember to keep them cool and moist with a daily sprinkling. Do not let them hatch until their natural food is ready. Predatory species must be separated quickly, as brothers—and sisters—may display decidedly unbrotherly behavior.

And then prepare yourself for the inevitable: insects are generally short-lived. Just as you get to know them, they mate and die, leaving you with a clutch of unresponsive eggs. Most insects, it seems, are orphans before they start.

Eggs do not always have the task of carrying a species from one year to the next. Each winter I am called upon to explain a veritable plague of insects in somebody's home. Usually it's a few thousand cluster flies—those zany creatures that congregate on your windowpane, fall down on the sill and spin around on their backs as if they had a case of vertigo. These harmless insects sneak into your house under the eaves, beneath the siding and even through your keyholes. They will leave quietly in the spring, but in the meantime you are in the fly-raising business, whether you intend it so or not.

Less often you may find yourself playing landlord to several hundred ladybird beetles—or ladybugs, as they are often called. Like the cluster flies, the ladybirds enter through any available opening. They, too, will go their way the following spring. However, in view of the current fad of buying ladybirds by the pint and releasing them to annihilate insect pests—

a process which may or may not work—it might be well to look into their habits.

Ladybirds, for all their attractive red and black coloration and roly-poly silhouettes, are about as voracious as the praying mantis—at least when they are young. Their tiny eggs hatch into startling grubs that look like caterpillars with thorns. These spraddle-legged larvae run among the clusters of aphids where their mother has conveniently placed them, slicing through their soft-bodied prey like a suburban lawn-mower through the grass on a summer weekend.

To raise your own ladybirds, it is important to have a ready supply of aphids. Aphids are a good source of food, since they remain obligingly in place on their twig until they are harvested by the six-legged little reapers. Be sure to put the twig in wet sand so that it stays green. And do keep the individual grubs well fed and separated or, like the mantis, they may start feeding on each other.

When they have attained full growth, the ladybird larvae will go into the pupal stage. In that state they remain quiet, like the cocoon of a moth, until they emerge about a week later. Still hungry, the first one out may make a meal of a late-emerging neighbor, although it is more likely to graze peacefully among the aphids if plenty are at hand.

It is best, at this point, to let it go free, as ladybirds often do not mate well in captivity. In fact, they will spend most of their time crawling on the glass of the vivarium, seeking to escape. But a liberated ladybird will launch itself on a handy congregation of aphids and soon leave several hundred replicas of itself to carry on its work.

In the ladybird family there is an errant cousin whose ways are reflected in its Latin name: *Epilachna corrupta,* the Mexican bean beetle. As the beetle's common name implies, it goes directly to the source of

65

nourishment instead of waiting for that nourishment to be processed through the body of an aphid. That source is the foliage of the bean plant.

Bean beetles in the form of eggs, larvae or adults can be harvested from the garden of some grateful farmer. You can raise these insects, and other plant feeders, by supplying their needs in the form of a few sprigs of their chosen food. Put the ends of the sprigs in wet sand in a vase. This keeps the foliage tasty and the sand will prevent wandering insects from drowning if they tumble into the vase. The vase should be surrounded with a cylinder of screening closed at the top; a useful idea in keeping other insects as well.

You can raise almost any insect by filling the basic needs for food and shelter. And you will also have the enjoyment of watching life unfold. The large caterpillar dressed in prison stripes on your carrot plants, for instance, will after suitable carrot-top meals and a brief pupation emerge as a magnificent swallowtail butterfly with black velvet wings ornamented with yellow spots.

Any large flying insect, by the way, should have plenty of room to spread its wings. And a moth cocoon or butterfly chrysalis must be firmly attached to some support—either by its natural silk tether or by a dot of glue. Otherwise the unfortunate insect cannot find firm footing to pull itself free of the pupal case. So if the pupa should fall from its attachment on a twig or leaf, you must glue it back in place.

Not all plant feeders need fresh greenery. One of the best known of hand-raised insects is the mealworm. Once regarded as nothing but a pest in feed stores and grist mills where it ate its way through the grain, the mealworm gained new life when someone discovered that it was easy to raise and good to eat—at least from the point of view of toads, frogs, reptiles and other creatures. So, with the popularity of pets at an all-time high, the mealworm's future is as bright as its past was checkered.

To raise your own mealworms, either for food or fun, all you need is a wide-mouthed quart jar, plus a box of cereal bran. Put about two inches of bran in the bottom, then place a double layer of moist—not wet—burlap or other coarse cloth on top of the bran. Cover with two or three inches more of bran. You will probably not need additional water, for mealworms manufacture water from the chemicals in their food.

In case there is no grist mill handy, and if the local supermarket refuses to let you prowl out in back among the cereals and flour, you can get a starter batch of mealworms at the pet store. Place a dozen or two of the inch-long, waxy-yellow worms in the bran. Add two half-inch cubes of raw potato weekly for moisture. The potato adds a little variety, too, which even mealworms can use.

The worms will eat and moult until they can grow no more. It's a slow process, taking four or five months from egg to adult—which doubtless explains why more people don't raise their own mealworms in this hurry-up world. When they are ready to pupate, the worms gather between the layers of burlap. The resulting beetles, known as darkling beetles, produce scores of eggs—and you'll find yourself in the mealworm business.

There are other insects that are not at all fussy about their food preferences. The common earwig will practically raise itself, as many a despairing housewife will agree. This half-inch, chocolate-brown insect comes to us from Europe. It is quite impressive, with its curved rear appendages that look like a wicked pair of tongs but are actually quite harmless.

The earwig derives its name from the mistaken belief that it gets into the ears of sleeping people. When we were quartered in somewhat less than plush accommodations during World War II, these inquisitive creatures became part of our lives. They crawled on the floor and into our bunks, to the horror of some of my finicky buddies. Actually, they were more attracted by the warmth and the possibility of a few K-ration crumbs than the chance of a sneak attack on an available ear. But a good legend dies hard.

Earwigs are interesting pets in themselves and when grown make good food for a variety of other creatures. They can be raised on chunks of potato, apple, raisins —and K-ration crumbs, if you have them. Like the praying mantis, they undergo a gradual growth, rather than a series of startling changes, like the caterpillar. In this respect they resemble one of the most durable of all insects—the common cockroach.

You've got to hand it to the ubiquitous roach. Not only has it made its way nearly from pole to pole, but it also somehow finds a home in high-rise apartments, subways and even ships and planes. Cockroaches watched the coming of the first dinosaurs and, scientists say, they may well be present at the demise of man. They can easily withstand radiation that would be lethal to humans, and they are able to survive on almost anything edible and not so edible—from the dregs in an old beer bottle to the glue in the binding of a book.

About the only rule the roach lays down for its existence in your menagerie is that there be plenty of moisture and a chance to hide. You can feed it almost anything: fruit, bread, bacon, peanut butter. Then, as you watch and learn, you may begin to understand how it has survived some three hundred million years.

You'll discover that the cockroach has developed the perfect incubator for its young. The female carries the egg case around until it hatches. As soon as the nymphs burst from their cradle they are off and running. If, in their zest for life, they dash into that vivarium pool, there is no harm done. They can swim from the day they are born. Many roaches can even tumble over on their backs and keep right on running. Their legs are constructed in such a way that they can push themselves along, rather than helplessly clawing the air like an overturned beetle.

You will learn these and many other interesting facts in studying this undersized—and underestimated —neighbor from the basements and waterpipes. You'll discover its exquisite radar system, for instance—delicate cerci that project to the rear and are so sensitive to air vibrations that the roach can dart ahead of a pouncing cat. You will also learn that, despite the surroundings in which it lives, the roach, which frequently licks and preens itself, is scrupulously clean.

Regarded as a pest in many parts of the world, but of equal interest, is the insect known as the white "ant" or termite. If you pull apart an old log or a piece of rotting lumber, you may very well find these pale creatures at work. The worker termites are smaller than a grain of rice, but the queen termite is several times their size. To start your colony, gather a number of termites and, if possible, the queen, together with a good supply of the decaying wood. Place them in the vivarium and cover the outside of the glass with dark paper or aluminum foil.

The termites will make galleries through the wood and you will see many of them running along the glass if it is kept dark. You can examine them under subdued light and discover that your wooden wonderland has several kinds of inhabitants. In addition to the workers there are soldier termites—big-headed and strong-jawed. There may be winged termites, too. These are reproductive forms that will someday fly away to start new colonies.

You may even discover that your pets have "pets" of their own. Tiny beetles, mites, and spiders can sometimes be seen running along the galleries. They are, of course, not really pets but they are tolerated by the industrious workers and the scimitar-jawed soldiers. They feed on smaller organisms in the nest and even a young termite or two when nobody's looking.

By the way, there is little danger of accidentally infesting your home by having a condominium of these creatures in the living room. Termites need constant moisture, and any strays would die soon after leaving the nest.

Termites and cockroaches are an exception to the general rule that most insects are orphans. Some termite queens have been known to live for forty years—far longer than any of their progeny. You will also find that in the societies of ants and bees, too, the queen often out-lives her offspring.

To start your own ant colony, dig up an anthill and, if possible, try to find the large queen. Place her with a few dozen workers and some earth in a formicarium. This is a scientific-sounding name for two panes of glass separated by half-inch wood strips around the edges. A few gaps, loosely plugged with paper toweling, are left in the wood for ventilation and as a means of caring for the colony. On the inside, near one of the holes, place a bit of sponge, which can be moistened daily with an eyedropper. An eyedropper in another hole can be used to supply a few drops of the daily ration of water, honey, melted butter and a little egg white. Add a crumb of bread or a fresh-killed insect now and again for variety.

Keep the formicarium covered with foil or dark paper except when you are watching the ants. They will fashion their abode into galleries, chambers and warehouses. The tiny white eggs will be groomed and carried about by the workers, as will the larger grublike larvae. Such attention prevents the growth of mold and parasites. The grubs turn into cigar-shaped co-

70

coons—the "ant eggs" that are frequently sold as turtle food.

Probably the most spectacular of the insect cities is that of the honeybees. Biological supply houses sell observation hives. These are glass-walled colonies of a few thousand bees plus a queen. You'll recognize the queen at once, for she is larger than the workers. Like most queens, her life is not her own; she is the center of a constant circle of attendants.

An observation hive is approximately the size of the lower half of a small window. It has an opening at one corner through which a tube can be extended. Place the hive against the window on the inside of the house with the tube leading to the outdoors through the small opening. Now you are ready for hours of entertainment.

To me it is one of the most thrilling sights in nature to watch a worker bee depart, circle to get its bearings, and then zoom off into the unknown. Back it comes in half an hour, loaded with pollen and nectar. Among all the fields and trees and buildings and windows the tiny creature unerringly returns to the tube leading to its home and life.

The activity of the hive is endlessly fascinating. You can watch the queen lay her eggs, one in each cell of the wax comb. The workers care for the larvae, feeding and grooming them. You'll see a division of labor with some workers performing as nurses, others as builders, still others as makers of honey and "bee bread"—a mixture of pollen and honey.

One sunny afternoon I sat in a friend's house, absorbed in watching his observation hive. I jotted notes and took a few pictures with the close-up lens of my camera. Then I realized that my friend's two daughters had joined me. "It's kind of fun to watch them, isn't it?" I said.

Little Jeannie responded with perhaps the highest

tribute that could be paid the antics of the living world in the twentieth century:

"It sure is, Mr. Rood. Almost as much fun as watching TV."

6. The Little One
That Didn't Get Away

John White and I felt guilty all that day in school. We'd
gone fishing the night before and come home about
midnight with a fine catch of bullheads. These be-
whiskered creatures, belonging to the group known as
catfish, grew in profusion in a little pond near my
home. We'd dumped them, still alive, into a burlap
sack, tossed the sack in the back of the pickup truck—
and promptly forgotten them.

Now, the next day, the sun shone brightly down on the bullheads while we thought about a night's fishing spoiled through our carelessness. Bullheads are delicious, but not after they've sizzled in the sun all day. However, it was four miles from the school to my home, and there'd be no going back until after three in the afternoon. So John and I tried to absorb what we could of civics and chemistry and English—while thinking of those eleven ripening bullheads.

When the bus let us off at my house, we glumly made our way to the back yard. Yes, there was the sack, containing our eleven bullheads, just where we'd left it.

But much to our surprise we discovered that the sun had apparently had little effect through the damp cloth. Catfish are incredibly hardy, and nine of the eleven captives were still alive. Out of water for fifteen hours, they had been able to absorb enough oxygen through their moist skins to keep body and soul together.

We hastily dumped the survivors into a tub of water. Then, deciding not to submit them to any further indignity, we trundled the tub back to the pond. There we released the whole batch.

They swam gratefully down into the muddy depths, all but the smallest one, which floated right back to the surface. There seemed to be no other choice than to take him home with us in the tub. When we got him to the house he had rallied considerably, so we decided to see how long we could keep him.

"Lucky" stayed with us for more than a year. During that time he doubled in size. We put him, tub and all, down in the cellar in winter and out under the lilac bush in spring. And it was under the bush that the durable catfish's luck ran out. An itinerant raccoon, possibly attracted by spilled bread crumbs—or perhaps merely groping in the water out of curiosity

—came across our piscatorial pet. We discovered the tragedy when we went to feed Lucky, and found nothing but a few of his remains at the base of the tree where the 'coon had hauled him to finish him off.

Thus ended my first experience in keeping native fish in a homemade aquarium. And, although I lost the tub's twelve-inch inhabitant, I still count it a success. Since then I've had dozens of other aquaria, liberally festooned with such gadgetry as airstones and charcoal filters, breeding traps and immersion heaters. Yet I believe I'll never get more pleasure than I did out of dropping bread and worms down into that froggy mouth as it obligingly came gulping to the surface when I tapped the tub.

The point is that an aquarium is not all that difficult to set up and maintain, and the keeping of fish is becoming increasingly popular. One aquarium manufacturer contends that there is a fish tank in one out of every twenty living rooms, but his figures may be suspect: after all, he promotes and sells the things.

Nevertheless, there are millions of people who, at least figuratively, are tied to the tail of a fish. The lure of the water is a siren call. We hear it and heed it at the beach, in a boat, even in a fishbowl. With only three percent of our country left in a primitive condition, the little tank will become ever more important, particularly in urban America. A miniature world can be set up in a few gallons of water; a world that can be maintained with only a few morsels of food each day.

How do you go about setting up your own personal aquarium? There are dozens of books available in pet stores and book stores to help you. These books go into more detail than we can provide in a single chapter, but the main points will be the same. Here are a few suggestions on caring for fish whether it's an intransigent catfish or a brace of guppies.

First, even though the word was used a few paragraphs back, try not to think in terms of "fishbowl." This word brings to mind that unfortunate creation resembling a sphere with a slab taken off the top in which, traditionally, a goldfish spends its life swimming in circles.

While the fishbowl has the advantage of cheapness and strength without supporting framework or cement, it has a number of drawbacks. It is hard to clean. Its spherical shape tends to make it topheavy and easily tipped. You must look at the fish from above—which is generally the least interesting aspect—or from the side, where you get a distorted view because of the curve of the glass.

Most important, however, the fishbowl presents a reduced water surface for oxygen supply. The narrow mouth of the bowl allows for very little air exchange, especially when it is filled nearly to the top. So if you must use a spherical bowl, fill it little more than half-way, to present the greatest possible area for air absorption. If you fill the bowl too full the fish will spend their time gasping at the surface. Then you will need an aerator to circulate the water and pump it full of oxygen.

Better than the old-fashioned fishbowl is the straight-sided aquarium. This familiar "tank" now comes in a variety of shapes: rectangular, square, or even six-sided. There is one slim tank that can be recessed into a wall, and another that is fitted within a massive picture frame. When this latter tank is placed on a shelf the picture frame hides the shelf and gives the appearance of a heavy-framed, living picture hung on the wall.

There are even three-sided tanks to fit in a corner and long, squat tanks to fit in a bookshelf. In all of these the straight sides allow an undistorted view and a wide air surface.

If you're the do-it-yourself type you can fashion your own tank from plate glass and aquarium cement. A tank two feet wide by one foot high and one foot deep makes a good starter size. Directions for the building of the tank are usually given with the cement, or you can get instructions from a pet shop. One such guide is "Custom Build Your Own Aquarium," published for about 50¢ by the Dow Corning Corporation. You can obtain this guide by writing to Dow Corning's Consumer Products Division, Midland, Michigan 48640.

Dow suggests that, in constructing a tank of your own, you use a trick known to cabinetmakers and model makers who need a temporary method of holding one sheet of material at right angles to another. The idea is to do the work on a level counter that meets a vertical wall, or place a sturdy, flat table against such a wall. Then, as cement is applied to each edge of the base piece, the corresponding upright side can be set in place and gently braced against the wall.

When all edges and corners are done in succession, an extra layer of cement is applied at all points along the inside. Then the aquarium can be tied or taped while the cement hardens.

Some cements, such as Dow Corning's Silicone Rubber Aquarium Sealer, are self-supporting and need no further strengthening beyond a 48-hour period in which to cure. All smears and extra blobs of cement are best left to harden. They can then be shaved off and scraped cleanly away with a razor blade.

Any aquarium should be washed before it is used. A teaspoon of ammonia to a quart of tepid water makes a good cleaning agent. Rinse the tank thoroughly in three changes of water. Drain and place it in its final location while it's still empty. Put it where it will get plenty of light but not direct sunlight. And be sure it's on a solid support; each gallon of water weighs eight pounds. Now fill it a third full with pond water. If no pond water is available, use tap water that has stood in the air for at least 48 hours to rid itself of chlorine or other harmful inclusions.

Add well-washed aquarium gravel or coarse, clean river sand so the bottom is covered to a uniform depth of about two inches. Double the depth if you plan to have a clam or mussel bulldozing through the sand. Slope the sand toward the front so waste material is easily seen and removed. Add more water until the tank is half full, pouring the water onto a floating sheet of paper so as not to disturb the material on the bottom. Put in a few rocks for atmosphere, and your tank is ready for planting.

Aquatic plants, for some reason, are apparently doomed to labor forever under weighty scientific epithets. Instead of a nice descriptive name such as featherleaf, for instance, one plant is solemnly known among aquarists as *Myriophyllum*—which, when translated, as you may have guessed, means "featherleaf." And if you walk up to an aquarium enthusiast, intoning such passwords as *Vallisneria, Elodea* and *Cabomba*—you will immediately be admitted to The Club. But it's plants such as these that you'll need to put in your tank. Mention their names in any aquarium store, accenting the next-to-last syllable in true scientific fashion, and you'll get what you need even if you don't recognize it.

Or, as an alternative, you can simply visit a local pond and uproot a few unpronounceables for yourself. Almost any underwater green plant is good, no matter what you call it. You'll want to quarantine these for a few days after you plant them in the tank, however, as they might have a retinue of camp-followers such as predatory insects or leeches. But, then, it's a good idea to let any newly planted aquarium establish itself before populating it with fish and other animals.

The mistake you're most likely to make at this point is to introduce too many plants. The plants will multiply rapidly as they utilize the wastes from the animals, so it's better to go slow. It's easier to add more than to uproot those that have already been planted. Depending on size, one medium plant per gallon of water is usually sufficient. Put taller plants in back, shorter ones in front. Long, slender kitchen tongs, by the way, make good aquarium planters.

Now, after you finish filling the tank, allow it to settle and age for about a week. Then you are ready to introduce the animals. Here, again, your enthusiasm can get the best of you. Be sure your fish and other animals are compatible. Otherwise you're liable to precipitate a finny free-for-all. Put half a dozen tadpoles in with a harmless-looking dragonfly nymph, for instance, and you'll have *no* tadpoles in a few days; just a harmless-looking dragonfly nymph. And, in case you're interested in native fish, be sure any companions you choose for a pike or a pickerel or any other predator are larger than he is. Otherwise he'll do them in, one by one.

How many fish should a fish tank hold? That depends on the size of the fish—and of the tank. A good rule is to allow one inch of fish per gallon of water; ten guppies in a ten-gallon tank if you're interested in exotics, or five two-inch native minnows if you prefer local talent. My foot-long catfish, for example, could have shared his twenty-gallon tub with an eight-incher.

The allowable number of fish depends on what else is in the tank. A clam or mussel is pretty large, but it's also pretty lethargic, so it's worth only a couple of inches of fish. In fact, it feeds by filtering small water organisms through its siphons, so it helps to tidy the tank. Pond insects use about half the oxygen needed by the more active fish. Snails are less demanding, too. The pulmonate snails even breathe air, taking it into a cavity beneath their shells and prowling around underwater until the air is exhausted. Some of them change their air while still submerged, poking up a slender breathing tube like a snorkel.

Few of these creatures can withstand foul water, however. A single dead plant uses up oxygen at an alarming rate as it decays. The decay bacteria release harmful substances into the water, compounding the problem. The buildup of these substances causes the fish population to seek air at the surface. If the situation really gets out of hand, every snail that is still able to travel climbs out of the water until things are more hospitable. The untimely demise of one of the tank's inhabitants adds to the woes of the others. Uneaten food quickly spoils, too; in fact, it is the single greatest cause of aquarium pollution.

On the subject of food, the kind and amount you provide will depend on the fish. Small fish will do well on the better commercial brands of fish food, available in pet shops. These contain dried plant and animal material. Add live food to the diet twice a week: finely chopped earthworms, or small organisms such as Tubifex worms sold in pet shops. You can also buy daphnia, the water flea. Daphnia has an added virtue in that it scoops up bits of debris as it swims, thus keeping the water clear. Or if you feel like collecting your own live food, pour a few pails of pond water through the fine mesh of a nylon stocking. The material you strain out will provide a veritable smörgasbord for any fish in your tank.

You also can find food in old tin cans and pools of stagnant water. Such spots are great breeding places for mosquitoes, and it takes a singularly aloof fish to resist the seductive wriggle of a mosquito larva. By harvesting the contents of an abandoned six-pack or the interior of an old rubber tire, you not only evict a few dozen mosquitoes but you also provide your tank with a valuable source of fresh food and vitamins. If you then take the cans or the tire to the rubbish heap, you are cleaning up the landscape—and that's all right, too.

Even the larger fish will snap up mosquito larvae. They will also feed on earthworms—whole, or in parts —plus pieces of chopped heart, liver and lean beef. Junior food chopped spinach or a bit of boiled lettuce will add the necessary minerals and will help lessen attacks on that greenery you so carefully planted.

Feed your fish once a day. Give them only enough food to be cleaned up in five minutes. If some is left over, feed them a little less the next time. Since some food is bound to drop to the bottom, enlist the aid of a natural cleanup crew. Many kinds of snails are good at this job. So are tadpoles. Both of these animals will sometimes dispose of the carcass of a fish or other creature, as well.

One of the best sanitation engineers is the lowly catfish. If your aquarium is composed of native species, add one more—a bullhead or other local representative of this whisker-faced family. Those sensitive barbels, or "feelers," caress the bottom gravel, somehow smelling or tasting the good among the gunk. And to a catfish, almost everything seems to be good. A healthy "cat" is a living vacuum cleaner, nuzzling through the debris with such enthusiasm that it sends a cloud of ejecta up behind itself like the discharge from a snowblower.

Now, with the scavengers doing the janitorial service, you have the makings of a well-run aquarium. The animals consume food and oxygen, leaving behind nitrogenous wastes and carbon dioxide. Plants use oxygen, too, but produce an excess of the gas as a byproduct of their daytime activity. They utilize the wastes from the animals, transforming them into edible leaves and tissues. Thus the plants help the animals and the animals help the plants—with the scavengers rummaging through the leftovers.

A well-balanced aquarium needs no further help from you. Indeed, one pet store in New York featured a tank, sealed with tape, that had maintained itself without a breath of fresh air for more than twenty years. Dimly seen within its algae-encrusted interior were a few small fish, some snails and a plant or two —all descendants of the original inhabitants. So sometimes an aquarium can support itself, recycling its food and oxygen, without human intervention.

Most of the time, however, tanks are far out of balance. There are too many animals compared to plants, with a resulting lack of food and oxygen. Here, of course, is where the need for daily care comes in. The oxygen supply is increased by means of an aerator, which releases bubbles in the water and creates a current that constantly exposes a new surface to the air. A filter—often run by the same pump that operates the aerator—removes excess wastes. And you add a necessary boost of energy daily with your offerings of food.

One constantly asked question is, "How often should I change the water?" The answer is that it should be changed only when it needs it—which may be never. Indeed, the less you tinker with the water supply the better. Aquatic animals alter their own environment as chemicals from their bodies are released into the water. They fashion their surroundings to suit themselves, so to speak. Then, just as they have adapted things to their needs, you come along and dump out the comfortable fluid. If your filter and scavengers are in good shape and you're not too heavy-handed with the food supply, the only water you may need to add is enough to replace that lost by evaporation. And with a glass plate on top of the tank, this may be only a few ounces a week.

Of course if you have a major catastrophe and the water becomes foul, the only way to clean up the mess may be to start all over. Place the plants and animals in water in a shallow container such as a clean dishpan. Then rinse the tank and its gravel thoroughly with plain water. Do not use soap or detergents, as they may leave harmful residues. Fill the tank with new water, replace the plants, and let it age as before; two days or more.

When you reintroduce the fish to the aquarium—or when you put any fish in new surroundings—let it get used to the temperature gradually. Dip the fish, along with enough water to maintain it, into a small container, such as a clean plastic bag. Float the bag in the new aquarium for half an hour; this will allow the temperature on both sides of the plastic to equalize. Then open the bag and allow the fish to swim away at its own speed. Or persuade it to leave, if necessary, by carefully upending the bag. If you're putting in a brand new fish, sneak it into the tank after dark, so the other fish will not bully it.

So far, most of the inhabitants of your tank have been spoken of merely as "fish" or, at best, "animals." Actually every major animal group has aquatic representatives and some may be far removed from the finny, scaly vertebrates known as fish.

Perhaps the new arrival is a diving spider, for instance. This creature puts on a fascinating display as it builds an underwater web and furnishes it with bubbles brought down from above. Or maybe it's that crustacean clown known as a crayfish, which reaches for a chunk of liver with a few of its ten legs while uprooting your plants with the others. Or, you may have a leech entrusted to your care. The leech is a distant relative of the earthworm and one of the most graceful of all swimmers as it undulates through the water toward the shred of beef you have provided for its suction-cup mouth.

Perhaps your guest is merely a boat-shaped bug—complete with keel—that insists on swimming upside down. Appropriately enough, it is known as the back-swimmer. Nor do its surprising habits stop there; as it paddles itself through the water with a pair of oarlike legs you may hear a distinct squeaking sound, as if something needed oiling. This, apparently, is back-swimmer language for "I'm available." And it seems to get results with the opposite sex. These fascinating underwater rowboats are found over almost all of North America.

Many aquatic insects are predatory, or at least scavengers. Since the group contains few strict vegetarians the matter of feeding your six-legged submersibles becomes largely one of supplying fresh meat. This is easily done by holding a small piece of lean beef or liver in front of the insect. Gifted with a superb sense of smell, the insect readily takes the food—even if it arrives at the end of a broomstraw or a pair of forceps, and submits uncomplainingly to being seized.

Your glass menagerie may include a few of those insects known as case bearers. These larvae of the common caddis fly look like underwater caterpillars. They surround themselves with bits of wood or tiny pebbles glued together to form a protective tube. Sometimes they will cement a small abandoned or still-occupied snail shell to the tube. There are even tales of caddis larvae in Rocky Mountain streams with intriguing bits of glitter in their armor—gold nuggets they have picked up somewhere in their wanderings.

Your aquanauts, no matter what their species, are full of surprises. Just watch as some water creature drifts idly near a dozing newt or salamander. There's a snap—too swift for the eye to follow—and the water creature has disappeared. The only clue as to where it went is a slow, deliberate swallow from the still-dozing salamander. Or follow the fortunes of a small crustacean as it brushes against the hairs on the birdseed-sized sacs of the bladder-wort plant. The hairs trigger a trapdoor that swings open, and water gushes into the sac, sweeping the crustacean with it. The door closes on the hapless creature, which is soon benumbed and digested in its prison.

Fish themselves are endlessly fascinating. And not necessarily only the fancy tropical types. I'll always remember old Lucky bullhead, who used to lie at the surface of the tub so we could stroke his back with a blade of grass. Occasionally he'd make a grunting sound, which we took for a transport of fishy joy when we hit the right spot. And I'd be willing to make a small wager that you'll find as much color and personality in the irrepressible little punkin' seed sunfish as you would in any gilt-edged tropical fish in town. You'll pay a lot less for him, too.

The day may come when you are present at the birth of a few dozen—or hundred—small copies of your tank's inhabitants. Female goldfish may begin to spawn when a year old, scattering sticky eggs on plants and underwater objects where they are fertilized by the male. Other fish have different forms of nesting behavior. The male sunfish clears a circle in the gravel where the female will deposit her eggs. Then he becomes downright pugnacious, even attacking your intruding hand if it comes too close.

Livebearers hold the eggs within the body until they hatch. Then the young are released into the water, where they must instantly take up their own precarious lives. The common tropical guppy is especially accomplished in this respect, strewing young all over the tank every few weeks.

Such are the fortunes of aquatic life that most baby fish are snapped up by their voracious neighbors—and often by their unsympathetic parents—before they are a few minutes old. Abundant plant life in which the young can hide will help to preserve their lives until you can transfer them to a nursery tank. Many aquarists—and you may think them hardhearted—put a few prolific guppies in a community tank, where the unfortunate youngters serve as an unwitting source of live food.

The young fish often subsist on the yolk sac attached to their bodies for a few days. Then they begin to eat protozoans and tiny crustaceans. If you put them in a tank with plenty of plant life they will probably spend their time picking at the organisms attached to the plants. Babyfood spinach, fed sparingly, is good for small vegetarians, and pet stores have a variety of starter foods.

You can also add the contents of a hay or grass infusion or the screenings from a few gallons of pond water. But watch those screenings; some uncooperative creatures may object to being considered as food. By a simple shift in pot luck the main course may turn out to be a fish dinner.

If its metal framework and seams are resistant to the effects of corrosion, your tank can hold salt water instead of fresh. Coat the metal with a nontoxic paint if you're in doubt. Instead of plants with leaves and stems you will probably use algae such as sea lettuce for greenery. Marine aquariums, as they are called, are becoming more popular as the problems in keeping salt water are overcome. With modern air service, fresh seawater and marine life can be flown to a point hundreds of miles inland in a matter of hours. And since we know that only the water evaporates from a tank while the minerals remain, the seawater can be kept at normal strength merely by the addition of fresh water when needed.

It has been said that if life in fresh water is compared to the fog on a misty morning, then life in the ocean is like a plate of thick pea soup. The immense variety of living things in the sea makes the possibility of a marine aquarium a fascinating one.

Starfish creep on hundreds of tiny feet that look like suction cups. Sea anemones gently wave their innocent-looking tentacles, waiting to paralyze an unwary fish or to embrace a bit of clam you obligingly drop in that flowery nest of stinging arms. Crabs stalk past on slender legs, poking inquisitive claws into a partly opened clam or taking a nip at a passing fish.

Most of the life in your small oceanarium will probably be native to the shore zone, where the water is oxygenated by the waves. Thus you will need the constant services of an aerator. A cool environment is best; 60°F. or even less. Cold water holds more dissolved oxygen than warm water. Place the tank against a slightly opened window to take advantage of the outside temperature. Shield it from direct sun or your thermometer will go up instead of down. If algae grow on the side next to the window, let them grow. They will serve as a screen against the light. Besides, they'll give your tank that forty-fathom look.

One final reminder. Creative genius that you are, you can set up almost any type of watery world you wish. But, fresh water or salt, it will be far more successful if you try to duplicate normal conditions. Determine what type of plants and animals usually live together under a given set of circumstances. Then, if possible, wade out and collect a slice of life for your tank. Or, if you're ticklish about walking in the ooze, balance yourself on the shore while you slosh around with a dip net.

And so there you are, even if you live on the twentieth floor, with your own bit of the mysterious deep.

7. Wet Suits and Goggles

You and I are impulsive creatures. We sometimes speak without thinking and do things on the spur of the moment. We drop letters in the mailbox and then wish we could get them back.

We're often the same way with regard to our pets. We're not always logical about selecting them. This may be especially true with the scuba diving subjects of this chapter: the amphibians, otherwise known as frogs, toads and salamanders.

Every spring, when the ice leaves the ponds, we hear the welcome croaks and peeps that indicate that the amphibians are at it again. They are pairing off—the frogs to deposit jellylike eggs in masses or singly, the toads to leave their eggs in long strings, and the salamanders to carry on the race in other ways.

It is at this time that thousands of youngsters—and their trout-fishing, flower-seeking, bird-watching parents—joyfully head for the country. And when one of those masses of eggs is found, attached to some underwater object and poised to deliver a few score of tadpoles, chances are good that it will go home with the finder.

We have already met tadpoles in an earlier chapter. But the sight of that pregnant blob in the water is so challenging that perhaps a few further comments would be useful. After all, there's no telling when the next amphibians will arrive at your house, in anything from an old tin can to the pocket of some triumphant budding explorer.

Frog eggs are among the most satisfactory of all pet endeavors. You can transport them in the aforementioned tin can—or even in a handkerchief sacrificed to the occasion. Put them in a pan or wide-mouthed bowl, together with water and a generous helping of bottom debris. They will develop almost while you look at them. Within a few days those buckshot-size spheres in their gelatinous envelope change into little black commas that twist and turn excitingly, each in a small hollow prison of its own. And before you know it, they have wriggled free.

After hatching, the larval tadpoles, each sporting a pair of gills that project from the head like bushy sideburns, hang vertically for a day or so, absorbing the last of the yolk sac. Then for another day they nibble at the gelatin of the egg mass. So there need be no sudden desperation on your part to find food for them, as there would be with an orphaned bird or mammal. They do quite well, all by themselves.

About three to four days after they have hatched, the tads turn their attention to the debris around them. Nibbling with sandpaper lips, they gnaw at the algae and assorted organisms that coat underwater objects in a slippery, nourishing salad.

At this point it is a good idea to return all but a dozen of your small charges to the wild. Those that you do keep can be maintained in almost any standing water of a fairly permanent nature. By the end of the second week, your tadpoles have lost their fishlike shape and are beginning to live up to their name ("tadpole," literally, means "tail head"). The external gills have disappeared, and are replaced by internal gills hidden in the tad's portly body. The tads scour the debris constantly, their finny tails sculling them to some favored spot, after which they shimmy along in an underwater hula, rasping away with their busy lips.

Within the confines of a bowl, even a scant dozen tads soon run out of available food. But more food is as near as your kitchen shelf. Spinach leaves and bits of lettuce, boiled thoroughly to tenderize them, can give relief to that overworked bottom debris. A small crust of bread is relished, too. Sometimes tadpoles will chew away at a bit of lean beef or fish; after all, they are going to be carnivores when they grow up. But be sure to get rid of every scrap of meat that is not eaten in a couple of hours, or the whole enterprise will come to a smelly halt.

Under warm household conditions your tadpoles should begin to transform into frogs in about a month. This is another satisfactory point in their favor: tadpoles are so active and they change so rapidly that even an impatient child maintains interest. Almost before you know it, tiny helpless-looking hind legs appear at the base of the tail. The animal's figure alters, too; it's still well rounded, but you can begin to guess where hips and shoulders will be.

As the hind legs get larger, two buds begin to show at the front of the body. These buds mark the site of the forelimbs. Up to now the tadpole has drawn water

90

into its mouth, past the gills, and out a side exit, called the spiracle. Now one of the forelimbs inconsiderately elbows its way out through that spiracle. The tad must constantly pop to the surface, gulping air into a newly developed set of lungs.

At last the transformation is complete. The tail, which has been giving up its substance for the build-up of the legs, lungs and other organs, becomes ragged and frayed. Gradually it is reduced to a stump. The pucker mouth changes into the sardonic grin of the frog. The long spiral intestine of the vegetarian, visible like a coiled watchspring through the transparent body, shortens to a more purposeful length. Meat-eaters, it seems, require less attenuated innards than plant-eaters who must process all that roughage. Thus a carnivore has a proportionately shorter intestine.

And the frog, most definitely, is a carnivore. Remembering that you have to present him with moving prey, you poke a piece of beef at him with a straw, or allow an insect to walk within range of his vision. He will turn and sit bolt upright, facing his potential dinner. Then his mouth snaps open, and there's an audible *plop!* as his long sticky tongue flips out to bring in its prey. The bulging eyes blink hard, pushing onto the roof of the mouth and forcing the food down the gullet. Then the frog is ready for the next morsel.

The frog's preference for moving prey is ordinarily a sure method of getting food at it's freshest. I once knew a toad that took up a station nightly below a lighted window. There he gorged himself on insects that crashed against the window and fell toward his welcoming jaws. We discovered him when we got curious about the intermittent *plip! plip!* we heard underneath the window on a still summer night.

But insistence on moving prey nevertheless has its drawbacks. A frog will snap at a blowing leaf. Or, he will gulp down a piece of cloth on a string—a quirk that people sometimes employ in fishing for frogs at the edge of a marsh. One bullfrog in the water hazard at Bethpage Golf Course on Long Island gulped down a golf ball that came bounding toward him—and died of an outsized case of indigestion.

Barring such incidents, a toad or frog may be expected to live for half a dozen years. While stories persist of toads having been found alive after being buried for centuries in an Egyptian tomb, they are pure fabrications. It's just that a toad looks so ancient and wrinkled and warty that we think it must be of an advanced age. Not so, however. Depending on the species, a toad who lives beyond ten or twelve years is living on borrowed time—warts, wrinkles and venerable appearance notwithstanding.

Another tale that dies hard is that toads will give you warts. That dry, warty skin—which, by the way, is one way of telling a toad from his wet-skinned cousin, the frog—is tough and leathery. But it is by no means able to give you any kind of infection. The only creature that will get warts from a toad is another toad—by inheritance.

Still, there is one mild precaution to take when handling these creatures: the swelling behind each eye is a parotid gland that secretes an acrid-tasting substance. This is why a dog or cat that may pick up a toad will usually drop it hastily. It paws at its mouth in agitation and, from then on, usually treats toads with respect.

Incidentally, there *are* toads with highly poisonous parotid glands. For the most part they are tropical species, however. Some natives of South America squeeze the milky fluid from the glands of one toad and dip their weapon points into it. Result: poison darts and arrows. But the variety found in your garden or vivarium is not poisonous. Merely remember to wash your hands after a session with him.

Otherwise you may accidentally get a shockingly unpleasant taste similar to that of a metal spoon that has stood too long in mayonnaise.

And I speak from experience. I have tasted the spoon and the toad—both by accident.

Although your frogs and toads began their lives in water, they need a place to haul out on land once they have gained full growth. Indeed, toads can spend months without going near the water—a fact that may have been responsible for the Egyptian tomb myth. Toads must have a cool, dark hiding place, however, to conserve the moisture in their bodies. Frogs, of course, spend half their time in water. They absorb oxygen through the skin, which must remain moist to do its job. And both of them are at their amphibious best during a rain, when they come out onto roads and fields by the hundreds.

When I was a boy and had a large lawn enclosure populated with toads and frogs, a friend told me how to solve the food problem. Put an old piece of meat in the enclosure, he advised. Sure enough; it worked just like the chunk of banana that draws the fruit flies to feed the baby mantids. Insects, attracted by the smell of meat, flew to their doom by the dozens. The amphibian's flypaper tongue, attached at the front and capable of extending half the length of the body, seldom missed its target. The keen-eyed amphibians became so good at this that they'd pick a circling insect out of the air.

Tree frogs are accomplished acrobats when it comes to catching a meal. Launching out from his twig, a tree frog (such as the spring peeper) abandons everything to the task. He flings himself at a passing fly that he may spot on a tree trunk or between him and the next branch. He observes the speed and direction of the victim, so he often takes a "lead" on his target like a hunter after a duck.

Winging fly and widemouthed frog meet in mid-air. The rest is up to Stickytoes, as Thornton Burgess called him. Gifted with a suction disc at the end of each toe, the frog grabs for any kind of support. Sometimes he manages to connect with only one or two toes. He hangs there a moment, wildly clutching for a better grip—while trying to take a second gulp at the half-caught fly. Apparently falling holds no terrors for this featherweight; I've seen tree frogs make spectacular leaps in an elm tree with nothing but forty feet of space below.

Put tree frogs in a vivarium with a twig or two for exercise and homey atmosphere. As with all your creatures, try to make the scene as natural as possible. But remember that these amphibian aerialists are not very large. The spring peeper is only an inch long, other tree frogs scarcely larger, in spite of the impressive volume of their birdlike chirps. Thus they, or any small frog, should be kept separate from their larger cousins. After all, a frog jumps at anything that moves—and for a bigger frog, this moving prey could just as well be one of his smaller brethren.

When winter approaches, your pets will need to hibernate. If you have a cool cellar, you can put them in a box with a foot of soil and dead leaves. The box should be covered with a screen to keep them in, and to keep other animals out. The soil should be moistened at weekly intervals. It should be kept wet for the frogs, as they ordinarily would burrow down into the bottom ooze of a pond or swamp. There they hibernate, absorbing enough oxygen through their skins to keep alive.

If there is no cool cellar available, perhaps you had better let them go. While they will remain active at room temperature all winter, they may be indifferent feeders, even if you manage to scrounge up enough insects to keep them going. Then you may have to cram food down their protesting gullets—or watch them waste away to nothing. If you plan to release them, do so before the weather gets cool, so they can work out their own destinies.

There is one other recourse for the winter that I have used a number of times. All it takes is a few inches of space in the kitchen—plus an understanding family. Since under normal conditions frogs and toads spend a chilly winter, just put them into a box and sneak them into the refrigerator.

Push them into a back corner in case you expect icebox-raiding guests who wouldn't understand. Wet moss or crumpled paper toweling will be all you need, plus a cover to keep things from drying out. Then, with a little attention to moisture, your pets will keep at a nice, comfortable chilliness until it's time for the spring thaw.

Many of these same tricks can be used with salamanders. You can put them away for the winter, too. However, this is not necessary with the newt or pond salamander so commonly found in eastern North America. Under wild conditions the newt is slowly active all winter, spending long periods on the bottom, but occasionally changing position as one in a dream. In your temperate tank or vivarium, it will scarcely seem to note the passing of the seasons. It will creep up on a bit of meat or an unsuspecting water insect just as if it were June instead of January.

If their surroundings are undisturbed and there are plenty of plants on which to fasten their eggs, newts will breed in spring. The male is easily distinguished from the female by his thick, muscular hind legs. He uses these to clamp his mate in what would seem to be a paralyzing vise-like grip. During the breeding season two males may lock onto each other in a temporary case of mistaken identity. Things obviously get straightened out, however, for there is seldom a scarcity of newts, young or old. The four-inch creature with the olive-green back and yellow belly is one of our best-known amphibians.

A young newt is quite different from its parents. For years it was thought to be a separate species until we had a more complete understanding of its life history. After a larval existence in water, complete with external gills, the juvenile newt climbs out onto the land. It loses its gills and develops the lungs it will have the rest of its life. The smooth larval skin becomes roughened and brick red in color. Now it is known as the eft—the "red lizard" so commonly brought home by children who have picked it up off a damp road after a rain. Of course, it's not one of those scaly, swift reptiles at all, but just a plodding lookalike.

The red eft may spend a whole year away from water, wandering more than a mile from its native home. The startling contrast of its bright-hued body on a patch of green moss may actually be a warning coloration. Few creatures will disturb it. Once an animal has sampled the first red eft, and been repelled by a distasteful skin secretion, it leaves subsequent efts strictly alone. And when the eft, still inedible, returns to the water for its last year or two of life, the fish there have to learn their lesson, too.

In spite of its unpalatability, the eft (or newt) shares a habit with the rest of its clan. Like toads and frogs, salamanders periodically shed their skins. In the neat economy of nature the cast skin is recycled by being swallowed by its erstwhile owner. One of the more impressive sights of my backyard frogpool was seeing an amphibian industriously tucking its exterior into his mouth with both front feet.

There are about eighty species of salamanders, ranging over our continent. They come in assorted sizes, from two inches to more than two feet. They come in many colors, too, from the spotted and marbled salamanders with their yellow or white markings on a dark background to the red-backed and green species. There is the dun-colored *Necturus,* the mud puppy, a foot long, with ridiculously small legs and three pairs of red, feathery gills. There is also the Allegheny hellbender—a two-foot-long wrinkled creature with the general appearance of an old boot.

Most salamanders are secretive, hiding away in rotten logs or under stones. Like the frogs, they need to keep their skin moist, for it serves as an auxiliary lung. In fact, some have given up lungs altogether and breathe only through the skin. This need for secretiveness has given rise to a persistent myth about this little-known group. The myth is that salamanders can live in fire. And it's easy to guess how the story may have started. Old logs are frequently used as firewood. When the log gets heated, the salamander finds that its house is on fire. It wriggles out in desperation, slithering through the ashes in an attempt to escape. Since its skin is cool and moist, it may not be harmed by the experience.

You'll find the legend honored by some fire departments today—a salamander, emblazoned on the emblem, implying "we live in fire." And portable gasoline heaters are often known as salamanders—the fire breathers.

Of course your real-life salamanders must be kept cool and damp. They will suffocate within a few minutes if they are allowed to dry out. But they have remarkable powers in other ways. Blind cave salamanders can taste with the skin just as you can with your tongue. A severed tail can be regenerated. So can a severed toe. Even a lost limb may grow back into an acceptable stump, like the wooden leg of a sea pirate.

Gifted with these recuperative powers and possessed of a retiring nature that asks little more than a cool place to hide, the salamanders have eked out a living for the past hundred million years. Their cousins, the frogs and toads, have been on earth twice that long. So, slow-moving little sitting ducks that they are, they have outlasted the dinosaurs and mastodons and cave men.

Which, after all, is pretty good for a bunch of creatures that don't know enough to come in out of the rain.

8. Eve Had the First One

Ever since the Garden of Eden, reptiles have suffered from a bad press.

The snake has come in for most of the invective because of its reputation for being the fly in the idyllic ointment. But its relatives have not escaped, either. There is the lounge lizard, for example, who is known as a ne'-er-do-well. Then there is the loan lizard— twin brother of the loan shark who is held in such bad repute in our society. Again, there is the crocodile whose toothy jaws may cause the moisture glands in its eyes to overflow—these are the "crocodile tears" of the hypocrite. And the turtle, of course, is unbearably slow, both mentally and physically.

Luckily, the publicity is not all bad. There are thousands of pet owners who know reptiles for the marvelous beings that they are. They realize that these creatures are not cold or slimy or messy or any of the other horrible things that are associated with being a reptile. They know that smooth-skinned reptiles are satiny to the touch, like the fine patina on a piece of rare old furniture. Scaly reptiles have a rugged "feel" that's not unpleasant, either, like a beaded belt or a piece of burlap.

But to compare a reptile to an unyielding slab of wood or a floppy chunk of cloth is not fair, because it is vibrant and sensitive. When you stroke a snake or lizard it may press back in response to your touch. Once it has overcome its fear of humans—and you have conquered yours regarding reptiles—it lies complacently, seeming to enjoy the warmth of your hand. Reptiles are not really cold blooded; their systems are merely unable to store up heat as ours do, so they must absorb warmth from their surroundings. A lizard on a sunbaked stone may have hotter blood than you have.

There are many points you can learn about reptiles, if that cold-blooded monster thrust upon you is allowed to remain. You can watch the workings of the forked tongue of the snake and many lizards. The tongue is really a sensitive smelling device. It "licks" odor particles from the air and transfers them to a patch in the roof of the mouth known as Jacobson's organ. Here the smells are analyzed and sorted out: That boy is eating a hamburger. There's a cat in the corner. There goes a woman wearing My Secret perfume.

Doubtless such concepts as "hamburger" and "cat" and "perfume" are far beyond the limited powers of the reptile's brain, but its inquisitive tongue can receive such signals as "food" or "enemy" or "unknown." And its long body, lying in close contact with the earth, marks the beat of footsteps, the swish of the wind in the grass. A snake has no ears, but it "hears" vibrations just the same.

Still, it's a cold, insensate reptile that slithers through books and legends the world over. A lumpy heart of stone beats in his breast—at least in the 41st chapter of Job. He hungrily eyes the beautiful girl lost in the jungle, according to countless novels. And he hypnotizes helpless birds just as he hoodwinked Eve.

In real life, however, the reptile is none of these things. He amply repays every consideration you give him. His actions almost seem to border on affection. A garter snake I had when I was in high school would glide from the tabletop onto my lap. There he would lie for an hour or more, totally relaxed, while I read a book or did my homework. And a tortoise that crawled around the house for more than a year would often settle down to rest with his shell slightly cocked up on my shoe, just as a dog will lie down on his master's feet.

But enough about these creatures that "ain't what they ain't," as one youthful herpetologist sputtered in response to an adult's doubts about his indigo snake. Let's assume that you find yourself the overseer of a snake or a lizard or a turtle. Perhaps you got a horned "toad" through the mail ("they make wonderful pets," your souvenir-hunting friend was assured as he shelled out three dollars plus postage in Arizona). Or perhaps you rescued a turtle from the middle of a super-highway.

Or possibly you were the hero who saved a whole parking lot full of shoppers from the attacks of a vicious foot-long redbellied snake—as happened to an English teacher in Poughkeepsie who thereby got his name in the paper. Now comes the old question: what next?

This depends quite a bit on the animal involved. The first consideration, as usual, is to try to get a Slice of Life. The secretive snake needs a place beneath a stone or slab of wood where it can keep its secrets. A more forward species, such as the common garter snake, needs a small place to explore and a spot where it can bask in the sun. Climbing species will make use of a branch or other support on which to drape themselves, while burrowers will be at their best down where you can't see them.

A burrowing species, by the way, will do well in an old straight-sided aquarium. Provide several inches of soil similar to the type from its homeland: sand or loam or leaf mold, depending on the species. Place a piece of dark cloth or paper around the base of the aquarium. As the animal burrows it will probably keep going until it meets the glass. Then, if the glass is darkened, it will turn and follow it for a distance. By carefully removing the paper under subdued light, you can spy on your small guest without disturbing it.

Ordinarily, the average reptile is thought of as a creature found in dry surroundings, well away from water. This is only partially true. Into each reptilian life some rain must fall—or at least an occasional sprinkle of dew, even in the desert. Over most of North America some form of moisture is available daily. So provide a pan of clean water deep enough for your charges to take a dip—but shallow enough so they can get out again.

When I had my first garter snakes I discovered how much they needed water. To humor a friend who swore that the snakes looked thirsty, I placed a pan of water beside them. Then we both watched as the snakes buried their heads up to the nostrils. We could see their jaws moving as they drank for what seemed about five minutes.

Those snakes lived in an enclosure in the back yard near our door. My parents allowed them to remain on good behavior "provided they don't get out, Ronald—

not even the first time." However, the snakes were doubtless greeted with mixed emotions by the local parson, the bread man and contemplative traveling salesmen.

If you should build such a pen, make it round rather than angular. Then the snakes cannot pile up in the corners. It is surprising how high a snake can climb in a corner—nearly as high as its total length. But a two-foot-high, rounded wall should be ample.

Make the sides of the pen of some opaque material such as wood or stone, so that there will be some shade from all but the direct overhead sun. Extend the sides of the pen a foot or more below the soil to prevent underground escapes. Provide a few caves of rocks and boards for shelter, and provide a water dish big enough for the snake to wet itself all over. Then explain to the local cats and dogs that your pets are off limits.

Reptiles—especially the desert species—get much of their water from the food they eat. This works out well under normal conditions, but there may come a time when your charges refuse food. Take heart, however; it may not be a hunger strike. It's not unusual for reptiles to go days or even weeks without eating. To us warm blooded creatures, such a prospect may seem alarming, but to a snake or lizard or turtle there is no need for three square meals a day. After all, a lazy afternoon in the sun takes only a fraction of the energy that a bird spends, say, in searching for insects. Apparently reptiles get along on the principle that if you don't chase your food so hard you won't get so hungry.

You will have more success in feeding and general care if there is adequate warmth. For the most part, reptiles are creatures of the milder climates, and need a temperature at least in the 70's. Under wild conditions when it gets much below sixty, they often retire until things warm up. The borderline may be much higher for tropical and desert species, used to scorching temperatures. Give these species the warmth they need by means of artificial heat—a light bulb, or a location near a heat duct or sunny window. But be sure to provide some way to escape the heat. That glass enclosure can become a casserole in half an hour.

Along with warmth, you must make sure your snakes have a spot where they can be absolutely dry. Even water snakes spend long hours in the sun, basking on an old log or grassy hummock. And provide a place for the snake to shed its skin—a bit of wood or a stone or the crotch of a twig where it can rub its skin off once it has loosened.

As to food preference, a vegetarian diet is unknown among snakes. Most of them catch their food alive, overpower it and consume it on the spot. A few subsist on birds' eggs or insect cocoons—which are alive too, but obligingly stay in place. There are more dietary differences among the lizards and turtles, some of which are vegetarian, some carnivorous, and some just plain opportunists—taking whatever comes along.

Although snakes normally feed on living prey, the boundary between living and recently living is a bit hazy in the psyche of many of these reptiles. This is a break for you in your attempt to keep up a steady food supply for snakes that catch warm-blooded creatures. A bird or small mammal found by the roadside is often acceptable. It should be fresh, however. If a snake accidentally eats carrion it may turn up its toes.

Sometimes you can make feeding less traumatic for yourself and the potential meal by offering "disguised" chunks of beef or other meat. A friend of mine once was faced with the problem of finding food for his hognosed snake. It seems that the hognosed snake feeds almost entirely on toads and, while Jerry liked his hognosed snake, he also liked toads.

He solved the problem by catching a garden toad and placing it in a container with a few bits of meat.

An hour later he presented a piece of meat to his snake. The morsel was square-cut and unprotesting; it just lay there instead of trying to escape. But in spite of the supermarket smell the meat also smelled like a toad—and down it went. Jerry has fed such "frogs" to garter snakes and "mice" to milk snakes in the same way. The trick doesn't always work, and it shouldn't constitute the regular diet, but it helps to fill in the intervals between unfortunate victims.

Insectivorous snakes generally create less mental anguish for their human keepers. Most people are slow to get emotional over a mealworm or a grasshopper, and even may nod in grim satisfaction at the demise of a cockroach or a spider.

The prodigious size of the meal a snake can swallow is a source of endless wonder to me. The snake can easily eat something twice as big as its head. If we could do the same, we'd be able to down a watermelon —whole. The secret lies in the efficiency of the apparatus the snake brings to the task. Not only can its jaws become virtually unhinged, but the right and left halves of the lower jaw are loosely attached to each other at the chin. Thus the mouth can be opened to astonishing proportions. The throat of the snake is elastic, as is the body with its flexible ribs. The whole effect is like that of a stretch sock—capable of accommodating heroically to the job.

A snake's teeth curve backward, pointing toward the throat. After the reptile has seized its prey, it works one side of its upper jaw forward, securing a good grasp with those teeth. Then it works the other side forward. It does the same with the two halves of the lower jaw. In this fashion it "walks" its way over its unfortunate meal, which slowly disappears down that capacious throat. And, lest the tongue be injured somewhere along the line, it is safely tucked away in a special sheath.

The process of consuming a sizeable lunch may take an hour or more. With such a lasting mouthful the snake would seem in danger of suffocation. But there is another bit of apparatus for just such an occasion. Pausing in its labors, the snake projects a small tube from the base of the tongue. This is the end of its windpipe. A few deep breaths, and the windpipe disappears. The food may take days to digest. Meantime, the unwieldy bulge in its body could slow down the snake if attacked, so it retires to assimilate its meal. Thus it may go from one banquet to the next, without even a snack in between.

That sudden change in girth may bring on unexpected complications. One jungle explorer had captured a tapir—a South American animal somewhat like a pig—and placed it in a corral made of poles stuck into the ground. The next morning the tapir was gone. In its place was a large anaconda. The snake had slipped through the fence and swallowed the tapir during the night. Now, swollen with the still-undigested tapir, it was stuck between the poles on its way back out!

When your snake is about to shed its skin it seems to be suffering from some sort of malady. Its color becomes dull and lifeless. Its eyes turn foggy-white, almost opaque. It blunders into objects in its path; after all, that exploring tongue cannot tell it everything. The snake is irritable and touchy, perhaps snapping at you for the first time in its life. It reminds you of one of those "before" pictures in a health ad.

This unfortunate condition lasts for a few days. Then there's a change. The eyes become bright again and the color more vivid. This is due to a secretion beneath the skin. The skin loosens, first around the head. The snake rubs against some object to start the shedding process. Then, after further rubbing, it crawls out of the old skin, turning it inside out like a wet sock. Now the snake is glossy, alert and often has a keen interest in food—just the opposite of a few days before.

The old skin is a perfect mold, even to the eyes and nostrils. Perfect, that is, except for one thing. In the process of pulling itself out of the skin, the snake may have stretched and partially torn the moist tissue. When this happens the snake leaves behind a skin that's longer than its normal length. When such attenuated skins are found in the wild, people sometimes think that a record-breaking monster is in the making. Such stories often become more elaborate in the telling.

While length may be the outstanding feature of snakes, the primary quality of lizards is their alertness. Such names as "race-runner," "swift" and "dodger" tell of the general impression made by these reptiles. If you want to try your luck at catching one with a butterfly net, better be sure nobody's watching. The lizard will be gone before you're halfway through your swing. The best way to catch a lizard is to use a slender noose at the end of a fishpole. Lower the noose over his head with one hand while with the other you create a diversion by wiggling your fingers in the air. This may look kind of funny but it gets results.

But a lizard on a sunlit rock may not be the same creature in a vivarium. This is why heat and light are important. A good proportion of lizards need a temperature in the 80's, or even close to the 90's. They also need good, dry weather. Yet they must have water, even if they refuse to drink it.

These, at any rate, are the requirements for keeping such creatures as that mail-order horned "toad" and its less prickly cousin, the desert lizard. Plenty of sun is needed to duplicate the wide-open spaces of the Southwest—but always remember to have available shade. Although a glass plate on the vivarium would keep the temperature up, it would also raise the humidity. Better to provide a screened top; then the moisture can escape even if the heat does, too.

One way to provide relief from the burning sun is to have good, deep sandy soil for burrowing. There's another advantage to five or six inches of soil: you can plant a few cactus in small flowerpots and bury the pots in the soil. In that way the plants will remain in place instead of being uprooted by an energetic lizard. Sprinkle cactus, lizard and soil daily with water. Reptiles seldom drink from a dish—after all, pools of water aren't exactly commonplace in the arid lands where lizards are normally found. But dew is more familiar, and they will sample the glittering drops. Their skin absorbs a little water, too.

But hot-and-dry is not always the rule. Sometimes, as with anolis, the little Carolina chameleon, it's hot-and-humid. This changeable little pixie with the scarlet flash-patch under its throat thrives in lush vegetation where things are sticky-moist. There it will feed on flying insects, mealworms and an occasional earthworm.

Anolis, by the way, may set up a little territory of his own in your vivarium. He will claim it all until a rival appears. Then, after much flashing of that extensible throat patch and perhaps a few spirited fights, a truce will be drawn. But since possession is nine-tenths of the law, the intruder usually gets second choice: a corner, perhaps, or the most shaded side. So it's best—as it is with most creatures—to put the entire population into an enclosure at the same time. Then they are all strangers together and nobody ends up Odd Man Out.

Although it is called by the same name, anolis is only distantly related to the true Old World chameleons. Like them it changes its color from brown to green to gray by means of expanding or contracting pigment cells in its skin. But its action is determined as much by its mental state as by any attempt at camouflage. An agitated Carolina lizard may turn a bright green—which is fine on a leaf, but not on a tree trunk. And as it stalks its food it may go through its whole repertoire.

Like the Carolina chameleons, most lizards take living food. As with the amphibians, lizards may sometimes feed on smaller members of their own kind. So watch those sizes; if you don't, the lizards will. Mealworms make fairly acceptable rations, but their tough exterior may be a little rugged for a daily diet. Add a few flies, moths and other insects for variety.

A friend of mine has raised horned lizards for several years. He has found a good way to provide them with ants, at little effort and with outstanding success. He places a chunk of cake, meat or other food on the ground near an anthill. Then, when the food is covered with ants he lifts it up with tongs and drops it into the cage for his lizards. Or, sometimes, he places the lizard in a small screened enclosure. Setting the enclosure on the grass near the ants, he allows the lizard to snap away until it's full.

Looking somewhat like the lizards, but of quite different habits, are the crocodilians. My brother Jim and I had a young alligator when we were small. As I recall, we got it for a dollar ninety-nine and a handful of soap coupons. We faithfully followed the directions that came with it: a tub of water, a stone to haul out for basking in the sun, and a small bit of meat daily. We changed the water daily, too, for the instructions were explicit about cleanliness.

But our 'gator wouldn't eat. Tempting bits of liver and beef went untouched, as did the wiggling insects and earthworms with which we hoped to entice him. So we tried to forcefeed him. We got a chunk of meat down that cavernous white throat all right, but invariably we'd find it floating around in the water fifteen minutes later. So, since we didn't want to see him die on our hands, we took him to the lake in the local state park and regretfully released him. Of course this meant curtains for the semitropical saurian; the first frost of the Connecticut autumn doubtless finished him off.

Thus our embryo alligator farm was stillborn, and only much later did I realize what went wrong. The directions said to provide warm sunshine and clean, fresh water. We were careful to provide both. But they neglected to say anything about the starting temperature of that water. So our frequent cleanings resulted in a Louisiana native being dunked into a bath of frigid Connecticut spring water almost daily. Then, just as all that water finally got warmed up to where he could stand it, the sun went down.

Now that alligators and crocodiles are protected by law, the brisk trade in young 'gators is a thing of the past. But if, perchance, you should somehow get one even temporarily, be sure you provide the *whole* Slice of Life. Warm the water up before you put the alligator in it. It should be in the 80's, at least—about the temperature of somebody's forgotten tea.

The last, but one of the most popular groups of reptiles from a pet point of view, is the turtle. Every Christmas a few thousand young turtles are joyfully received as gifts. More thousands are bought in pet stores throughout the year, and there are still a few picked up on a walk in the country, or rescued from bewildered indecision in the middle of a roadway. Sandy road shoulders make good digging for turtles bent on laying a clutch of eggs, but the slow-moving reptile may lose her life before she gets that far.

Incidentally, if you do find a turtle crossing the road, and wish to help it to safety without getting involved for the next few months, the best thing is to place it across the road yourself—in the direction in which it was heading. If you put it back where it came from, it will doggedly turn around and start out again after you are gone. Turtles are not given to sudden changes.

If it becomes your lot to care for a turtle rather than place it temporarily out of harm's way, you have a rewarding experience ahead. Turtles, for all their plodding ways and gruff appearance, make interesting pets. Their slow, deliberate manner is fascinating, and the way they clump along with that astonishing shell never fails to amuse us. Furthermore, turtles do very well in captivity. Their wants are few and they are easy to feed and keep clean. Not only that, but I suspect that the care and feeding of the slowpoke turtle can be good therapy in our high-strung world.

The common pet store variety of turtle seems to get along quite well in a dish of water with a few smooth stones. In more complete living quarters, the water should be thick with plants, as young turtles spend their early lives among aquatic vegetation. There they find their food of pond snails, water insects and occasional tender leaves.

Most store-bought turtles are the young of the Troost's or "red-eared" turtle, and bear a red patch on either side of the head. Occasionally a map terrapin, Cumberland terrapin or other species finds it way to the checkout counter, too. The term "terrapin," by the way, is generally used for a fresh- or brackish-water turtle, while tortoises are those species that live on land. Huge oceanic turtles are called just that: turtles, and nothing else.

A young turtle—or terrapin, if you prefer—will do much better on a varied diet than on the dried "turtle food" sold in pet stores. Pieces of lean chopped meat, small insects, fragments of earthworm and shreds of lettuce will help round out the menu. Sunshine is fine, but a desk lamp for basking seems to do almost as well. While room temperature seems acceptable, the mid- to upper 70's will be better. A drop of cod liver oil on a chunk of meat serves as a good conditioner. Handle the meat with tweezers or the end of a tooth pick; your fingers make clumsy forceps for such delicate fare.

Most water turtles need to immerse the head completely in order to swallow. So your pool should be deep enough for normal feeding. Since turtles apparently can not be housebroken, the water will have to be changed daily. Once a week, as an added treat, fill a large dish with water. Allow your pet to have a good swim for an hour. And be sure the water is the right temperature, lest you repeat my dismal experience with the alligator.

Local pond turtles, such as the "sliders" or painted turtles, can be treated the same way as the high-priced varieties. Like almost any animal in captivity, they may suffer from an occasional malady. Keep a bit of cuttlebone or plaster of paris in the water to supply minerals to keep the shell hard. Eye troubles can be cured by plenty of sun plus a mild saline bath (one teaspoon of salt per half gallon of water) two hours a week.

The landed gentry among the turtles are the box turtles, upland turtles and tortoises. Fossils of box turtles have been found along with those of some of the last dinosaurs, so obviously their ability to close up their shell completely has been most efficient. Box turtles soon become tame and gentle, feeding readily on lettuce, berries, insects and lean meat. Live food in the form of earthworms and slow-moving insects will help enrich their vitamin intake. Although they do not need a swimming pool, they will make use of a shallow pan for wading and drinking on occasion. Plenty of sun is good for box turtles, but a shaded hiding place is also needed.

The true tortoises, with their stump-shaped legs and elephantine appearance are often neighbors of the lizards. Dryness is vital for them, just as for their speedy cousins. Most tortoises are vegetarians, and will subsist on lettuce leaves, celery tops, bananas and other fruit. Keep the temperature up for them, too—in the high 80's or low 90's—with plenty of sun. But, as always, be sure there's a cool place to hide.

I have had turtles of one variety or another for most of my life. They began with a small creature that lived all summer and autumn in a dishpan—and was panic-stricken when my folks put him in an aquarium, complete with two equally flustered goldfish, on Christmas morning. The turtle had never seen such creatures, and vice versa, and all three of them spent most of Christmas day trying to escape. Since then there has seldom been a time when there hasn't been one or more turtles around the house. And one of the questions, put sometimes delicately and sometimes bluntly by visitors, is "how on earth can you tell a turtle's sex?"

Really, it's not difficult. Many male pond terrapins have longer fingernails than the females. This is a fine way of making a distinction if you have one of each sex for comparison. But another way to discover what gender lurks under that armour is to turn the turtle on its back. And there, if you know how to interpret what you're seeing, is the answer. Male turtles often have a concave plastron, or under shell. The plastron of the female is usually flat, or even slightly convex. Further, the female's tail is short, with the vent almost hidden by the edge of the shell. The male has a longer tail, with the vent usually protruding well beyond the edge.

These seem like minor differences, but they have served turtles well for a hundred million years. Standard courtship behavior among many pond turtles is for the male to stroke the female's face with his front feet; hence the long fingernails. His concave plastron just fits over the top of the female's carapace as he mounts her during mating. His longer tail allows for adequate juxtaposition of the essential organs—and her slightly rounded underside allows for the development of a dozen or more eggs after the whole performance is finished.

But there is more. Once the female has received the sperm she is able to keep it, alive and waiting, in a special pouch, for months or even years. One captive produced fertile eggs four years after mating. She buried them, in typical turtle fashion, in about six inches of warm sand. So all the face-stroking and shell-bumping (a noisy preliminary that can sometimes be heard even under water) may not be necessary every spring. The turtle can often provide this year's crop of nestlings from last year's mating—if she can escape the bulldozer and cement mixer and get across the road safely.

With turtles, as with other reptiles, the coming of autumn brings a tendency to hibernate. Since food and warmth and sunshine are in short supply in winter, perhaps it is best to let them go to sleep. A container of moist soil, placed in the cellar or some other spot where it will not freeze, will make a good winter retreat. Cool a turtle down gradually; remember that approaching winter slowly is a normal part of that Slice of Life for your pet.

With luck—and a little of that T.L.C. to help things along—you may be able to do as well as my friend who has had a wood turtle in his home for seven years. And at seven years, things may just be getting started. After all, turtles have a reputation for longevity; they have been known to live for a century or more although the turtle with "4 B.C." carved on its shell must be regarded with suspicion.

And it's funny how reptiles will make their way into your heart, once you get over your first case of shudders. My turtle-owner friend says his family would be inconsolable if Electra ever gave up her reptilian ghost. And another friend, the editor of a large book club, has a seven-foot indigo snake that is so docile that even the secretaries in his office crowd around to pet it when he brings it to work with him. However, taxi drivers and subway patrons being what they are, he carries his pet in an innocent-looking satchel.

"Besides," he told me, "there are lots of innocent young girls working in Manhattan these days. I've got to think of them. After all, look what happened to Eve."

9. A Bird in the Hand...

Birds get into all sorts of scrapes.

They build their nests in strange places. They fly where they please, show up where nobody expects them, and eat what's bad for them.

Take those out-of-place nests, for instance. When a local merchant in Middlebury unrolled his awning early last summer he dumped four baby sparrows out onto the sidewalk. A construction crane started up after three weeks of idleness and cascaded a clutch of eggs down from its top pulley onto the workers below. Luckily, it was a hard-hat job, so there were no man-hours lost in shampooing. And a pair of distraught robins in our town watched three helpless fledglings go rumbling away in a dump truck at thirty miles an hour. The vehicle had been laid up for nearly

117

a month, and the birds had built their nest in a corner of the truck body.

Or take the birds that fly the wrong way. They may be drawn to the powerful rays of lighthouses and airplane beacons like moths to a candle. Every morning during spring and fall migration there may be from one to dozens of birds at the base of each tower. Overhead wires also take their toll. Birds thump into windows, too—apparently they see the reflection of trees and sky and attempt to fly into that phantom landscape.

Birds in unexpected places include the chimney swift fledgling that falls down into the fireplace. There is also the bird that gets trapped inside a sunporch and knocks itself silly trying to get out again. And then there is the half-dead bird washed up on shore, unlucky enough to have run afoul of an oil slick.

The birds that eat the wrong things include the half dozen robins that fed on poisoned earthworms. The earthworms lived in a lawn we sprayed with DDT in the early 1950's when this spray was being hailed as the sure cure for Japanese beetle. The following day there were the robins, shivering, staggering and dying.

Another unlucky bird was a duck brought to our wild-life management class in college. The duck had successfully evaded the hail of lead during hunting season, but was now dying a slower death: lead poisoning, brought about by feeding on the spent shotgun pellets in the bottom mud. Ducks, in typical bird fashion, swallow grit and hard objects for their gizzards, even if those objects are deadly poison.

A more fortunate bird, but an equally unhappy one, was a herring gull reeled in by my father on a fishing trip. The gull plunged after the bait just after it had been tossed out, and for the next few minutes we all were treated to an absorbing spectacle as Dad hauled his feathered prize down from fifty feet in the air.

Other than the loss of its dignity and a few feathers, however, the gull escaped unharmed.

Add to these unlucky ones the birds that are hit by automobiles, caught by cats and evicted by rainstorms that flood their eaves-trough homes. Top off the list with the thousands of young birds that have left the nest of their own accord but give the impression that they're alone, abandoned, and in need of care. There you have the unwilling subjects of this chapter—the birds that, for dozens of reasons, find their way into our hands and homes and hearts.

There seem to be no figures available, but I suspect there are nearly as many of these wild birds living— at least temporarily—in American homes as there are canaries and parakeets. But since we're concerned primarily with creatures that come into your home from the wild rather than from the pet store, this chapter will deal mainly with them. There are many fine books on the care of the more legitimate cage birds.

I'd better explain that word "legitimate." Although birds are a fringe benefit in the daily lives of millions of us, the law in many parts of the United States and Canada holds that it is strictly taboo to cage or confine an unharmed wild bird in any way. Bird feeders are fine, and to snatch a bird from the jaws of death is fine, too. But to keep a wild bird in the hope of making it a pet is something else again. Better check with local laws before you undertake an enterprise that may be officially regarded as shady.

Actually, even though there may be no local guidelines, it is well to remember that a native bird is as wild, in its way, as the other outdoor animals. No matter how we may humanize it and pity it as it seeks for a bit of food in a blizzard, we must realize that these circumstances are all in a day's life for a bird. True pity should be felt for the caged bird that cannot wheel away on the wind, or pour out its voice in song over its private acre of brushland, but must spend its life as a caricature of the wild creature it was meant to be. So, although you rescue and shelter a wild bird, consistent with local regulations, you must remember that you are doing it only for that day when it can be off on its own adventures.

The most familiar of these temporary boarders are the fledglings just out of the nest. There you are, walking along the edge of the city park, say, when a young robin chirps at you from a bush. Interested, you step over to have a closer look. That hungry mouth flies open and those wings flutter in an obvious plea for food.

"You're a cute little feller," you tell him. "Wonder where your mother is."

So you look around for his mother. But there's no mother.

"Hm-m-m," you say. "You're all alone."

You consider him for a few more minutes. Now, there's an orphan if you ever saw one. Or maybe he fell out of the nest. Those wings are certainly short; it must be days yet before he is supposed to learn to fly.

And so he goes home with you.

Or maybe it doesn't work out quite that way. Perhaps he arrived at your door unheralded, accompanied by some member of your family. And then, inevitably, the familiar question: what next?

The first move I would suggest is to retrace your steps. Put him back in his bush. Get far enough away so you don't frighten his parents, wherever they are. And don't worry about the human odor on his body; birds have a poor sense of smell, and he will readily be accepted. Then sit and wait—for an hour if you can.

That hour, long as it may seem, will be far shorter than the total time you'll spend with him if you turn your back on his home and family in favor of your home and family. A nestful of fledglings will scatter in several directions, and the hardworking adults may get around to each one only every quarter hour or so. They'll be able to find him easily by his insistent cries. But if he has been unattended for an hour you may, indeed, have a bird on your hands.

By this time your small dependent will most likely be ravenous. Young birds in the nest are fed every ten minutes or oftener, so your precautionary measures may have cost him a dozen feedings. And since young birds may consume more than their weight in food daily, he has some catching up to do.

Feeding a young bird is usually easy. Raise your hand over him and there's that open mouth—a perfect white-rimmed target. In fact, according to scientists, the mouth may be colored that way so the parent can see where to aim the food after coming from the bright sunshine into the comparative gloom of the nest.

So the "where" of getting food to him is solved. Next comes the "how" and the "what." For feeding, it is a good idea to use a pair of blunt forceps, such as spadelike tweezers with flat tips used by stamp collectors. These will not injure him as he enthusiastically downs your latest offering. An alternative utensil is a flat-ended toothpick that can be used like a little spoon.

As for the food itself, the needs of young birds are remarkably similar, no matter what their adult diets. The main requirement of that frantically growing body is for protein—good, tissue-building protein. Later he may become a seed or cherry eater. For now, however, he has wing muscles to develop and feathers to grow. Vegetable matter may be introduced for variety and as a source of water, since young birds in the nest do not drink liquid water. But plenty of protein is essential.

The protein can be meat, egg, insects or earthworms. The meat should be trimmed of all fat. Liver and kidney make good food and are rich in minerals. Like meat, they should be cut in pieces for easy swallowing. Quarter-inch cubes are generally about the right size.

Egg is especially good; after all, that youngster started out as an egg. But raw egg is messy, so it can be hardboiled and chopped. The chopped egg is mixed with just enough milk to give it the consistency of putty. Then lumps of it can be picked up with the tweezers. Or, for a more rounded diet, you can dip each piece of meat in beaten whole egg before feeding. This also serves to moisten the food for easy swallowing—although that eager little throat seldom has trouble putting away anything but crunchy dry foods.

If you have ever watched a robin preparing an earthworm for its young, you know that it thrashes the worm to a pulp. Then it stuffs the unlucky annelid into some willing beak. You can accomplish the same result less energetically by the use of a pair of scissors. Reduce the worm to half-inch lengths, dip in beaten egg, and serve. The recipe goes over fine, even though such a combination is not on the menu back in the nest.

An adult bird can swallow a beetle or a grasshopper without blinking an eye, but these insects have too much roughage for a nestling. So do the hairy larvae of the gypsy moth and the tent caterpillar—which, by the way, probably helps explain why these insects can flourish alongside a whole treeful of insectivorous birds. But caterpillars less richly endowed with fuzz, plus the many softer insects such as flies and small moths, add bulk and variety. More important, they represent the kind of food the bird is soon going to have to find for itself. So furnish an insect appetizer at least once a day.

The easiest food of all to prepare is canned dog food. Use the best brand obtainable; some bargain-basement dog foods are largely cereal and scraps. And, since it sometimes takes an interpreter to figure out just what the list of ingredients really says, it's best not to rely completely on this source of food. However, dog food is undeniably easy to keep and handle, so dip chunks of it in egg and it can do for most of the daily feedings. Like all food, it should be given at room temperature.

Once a day roll two or three food cubes in wheat-germ meal, and for variety, add a raisin or two that has been soaked overnight and drained. A cube of fresh banana, peach or tangerine (which is less acid than orange, and hence easier on those little innards) can also be given daily. These will add minerals and roughage, and keep the bowels in good working order. If the droppings get too loose, discontinue the fruit.

One pet book on my shelves suggests a few drops of brandy for diarrhea. Another prescribes the avian equivalent of a good tot of rum. However, as *spiritus frumenti* is in notably short supply in the world of nature, all my own young birds have remained teetotalers. Besides, your aim is to help the bird go off on his own rather than coming back for more.

A couple of drops of cod liver oil twice a week will help guard against constipation. So will a multipurpose vitamin drop every few days. Both of these should be added to chunks of food. They will help in the prevention of a number of maladies that can take a small life overnight. But they, too, are unnatural in a wild bird's intake. The most natural diet of protein, insects and occasional fruit is generally the best: that Slice of Life again.

Speaking of the slice of life, how often should a young bird be fed? Obviously, no matter how good your intentions, every ten minutes will wear you down. But baby birds are fairly adaptable; you can allow yourself the luxury of a whole half hour between feedings. Feed the bird just before each of your own meals; then you can enjoy a leisurely repast before you have to go back at it again. No need to feed before dawn or after sunset, either; most well-regulated birds get up and go to bed with the sun.

The amount of food given at each sitting—if poking food into a bottomless pit can be called a sitting —will be dictated by the bird itself. When it has had enough it will simply eat no more. No more, that is, for half an hour.

One more slice of alimentary life: baby birds, just like baby dogs or cats or humans, usually void their excrement right after eating. As my veterinarian friend, Don Gill, says, their food goes straight through. In a healthy young bird this excrement is often encased in a film of mucous, so it is released as a soft little capsule. The parent waits for the appearance of this capsule, takes it gently with its beak without breaking the protective coating, and flies away to drop it some distance from the nest. If you anticipate this natural timetable and prepare to receive the dropping on a small pad of tissue, you can keep the nest fairly clean. And it's no use hoping for a better day with more bowel control. Housebreaking is practically unknown among birds—even well-behaved adults.

The nest for your fledgling can be any small box or carton. It should have solid sides, as young birds are susceptible to drafts and may quickly develop pneumonia. A shoe box or quart berry basket lined with crumpled facial tissue is ideal. Do not use hay or straw, since these materials may carry organisms that cause respiratory disease. If the bird is still helpless and without feathers, keep a cover of facial tissue over the top for warmth. Beam a 40-watt bulb down from a goose-

124

neck lamp, if necessary, or place the shoebox on a heating pad turned to the lowest setting. A bottle or plastic jug filled with warm water will also make a good substitute mother. But watch that heat carefully; you want an incubator, not a smelter.

As the bird approaches full adult status you can cut the feedings down to once an hour. If he is not ready for such long fasts, he will let you know at about fifty decibels. Provide some kind of audible signal as he is fed—blowing a distinctive whistle, perhaps, or banging a plate. Then as you allow him more freedom, he can be called back for food and safety. Feed him, now, in a screened porch or other enclosure where he can exercise his wings. Leave excess food in a dish, so he can learn to pick at it.

To me it's a thrilling experience to raise some wild foundling from a tender youngster until it is full grown, and then watch it go off on its own. But this may not be easy with a young bird. You have been its sole support for weeks. That insect, hurrying along on a leaf, scarcely resembles a chunk of liver at the end of a pair of tweezers. And those ripening blackberries do not obligingly detach themselves from the vine and drop into a waiting beak. The bird has to learn about such things for himself.

What is needed now is a gradual release so the bird can begin to make the adjustment at his own speed. Feed him at the same place each time—a spot that can be opened to the outside, and to which he can return. Whistle or bang on the plate with each feeding so he associates the noise with the food. Then, when he comes in response to the call, you have an invisible cord that binds you to him.

The yard with all its sights and sounds will be strange to him at first. He will probably not go far from the familiar food station, and will come fluttering back when you call. But gradually he will go farther, picking experimentally at objects in the way that birds do. Some of these objects will turn out to be edible. Down the hatch they will go, thereby postponing the time when his hunger will bring him back for the hourly feeding.

Finally the day will come when he can make it on his own. He may return briefly when you call, give the food a half-hearted peck—then soar away without a backward glance.

We had two orphaned sparrow hawks that successfully made the transition from their fallen tree to the grasshopper-laden fields of our south meadow. Day by day, as flight time approached, we fed them at the picnic table in the front yard. We gradually weaned them from beef to grasshoppers, and were delighted one day when the female suddenly left her chunk of hamburger and nabbed a locust in midair like the little falcon that she was. It took the male a few more days to get his wings but then he, too, sought livelier prey than a strip of uninspiring meat.

They didn't forget us completely, however. Two weeks after we thought we'd seen the last of them we were having a picnic lunch with some friends. I had just turned my attention to the fire when there was a shriek from the table. I turned around to see our female guest staring in horror at little Akela, who had swooped to a landing on the top of her husband's head. Neither the husband nor the hawk was in the least concerned; they communed together in some unknown language for perhaps fifteen seconds. Then Akela sprang lightly into the air. A few strokes of his speedy wings—and we saw him no more.

Akela and his sister, Falco, were among our more successful efforts in caring for birds of prey. Too often these unfortunates are brought to us, full grown and wounded—"Somebody must've shot it, Ron. It's only an old hawk, anyway."

126

We thank our guest for the dubious honor of having to mend someone else's mistake in judgment. We give him a one-minute course in the vital role played by predators, and ask him to tell the hunter that hawks and owls are protected by law—in case he should ever meet that hunter again. Then Peg goes into the garage and gets out the bag of feathers.

Feathers, it seems, are almost as important to birds of prey as eating flesh. Hawks and owls need the natural scouring action of hair and feathers and bones to aid digestion. Excess roughage is rolled in a little ball, called a pellet, and regurgitated. A certain mouse, new to science, was discovered by means of its remains in the pellets at the base of a tree where a barred owl fed her young.

So we roll bits of liver and beef in feathers, and feed them to the fallen warrior. We give him a daily chicken head or neck as well. He may eat readily at first, but the result is almost always the same. Deprived of the skies and the freedom of its soaring flight, the magnificent creature is only half a bird. Appetite failing, he loses interest in life.

In desperation we bundle the captive up in the car and take it to Dr. Fred Mold at the Fairbanks Museum, eighty miles away. There, perhaps, the spacious flight enclosure will have a therapeutic effect while the hawk recovers. And sometimes it works. But, for the most part, the days of a stricken bird of prey are numbered, even if it has only been winged. The shock of contact with humans is just too great.

Young hawks and owls are a different story. They have not yet experienced the exhilaration of flight, and living near us is not nearly as traumatic. Should a young bird of prey be entrusted to your care, it will do well on bits of meat rolled in feathers or fur. Add an occasional chicken neck, pounded with a hammer, for roughage. Our old dog Jack once parted with a

few clippings of his coat for the benefit of a red-shouldered hawk who needed a little fur in its diet. A few shreds of undyed wool will do as well; after all, it doesn't need to be edible—it just needs to be rugged.

You have to realize in treating older birds that are sick or injured that they are not only suffering but apprehensive as to your intentions.

That miserable ball of feathers, hunched up on the lawn, may have eaten something inedible, or it may be in the throes of some avian disease. A soiled condition about the vent may be a sign of dysentery or it may indicate some internal injury. Without the services of a specialist it is difficult to diagnose the problem.

The best treatment, if you're not sure what's wrong, is to make the bird as comfortable as possible. Keep it warm; it can go into shock just like a human being. The average body temperature for a bird is somewhere over 100°F., so a light covering may be helpful. Place the covering loosely over the bird's head first; birds struggle less in the dark. Then making sure you do not interfere with its breathing, keep its head covered while you gently feel for broken bones or other injury.

In the event that a wing or leg is broken, the bird should have veterinary aid. If such assistance is not available, make the injured part as motionless as possible. Have another person hold the bird while you work. Use as little waste motion as possible, for movement of the jagged ends of bone will cause further injury. Bind a broken wing in a normal position next to the body. Allow the bandage to run beneath the other wing so the bird can use that uninjured member for balance.

A broken leg can be mended surprisingly well with a splint made of a popsicle stick or other flat piece of wood, plus some gauze and adhesive tape. The splint should extend from the upper thigh to beyond the reach of the toes, so the bird cannot rest any weight on the foot. While your assistant holds the bird, straighten the leg, gently pulling the bone to a normal position so the ends may knit together. Remember that any unnecessary movement on your part may result in further internal injury, so make every motion count.

Bandage the leg firmly to the splint. Make it as smooth as possible, because the bandage must stay on until the leg has healed, and there should be no painful wrinkles to chafe the skin. Wrap the finished product in adhesive tape to prevent the bird from picking at the bandage.

The bones of birds knit rapidly. Our young sparrow hawk, Akela, arrived at our house with a broken leg; we splinted it, and it was healed at the end of three weeks. Older birds may take a bit longer, but a month is usually enough.

The next question is how to care for your patient for three weeks or a month. Whether it has a broken bone or not, its early convalescence should be as quiet as possible. A large cardboard carton, with a rough wooden twig stuck through from one side to the other as a perch, will shelter the bird and keep it away from drafts. It can be darkened at first until its occupant becomes used to his surroundings. A covering of sand or fine gravel is used on the bottom; this can be raked over to cover soiled spots and washed when dirty. But be sure the covering is dried out before you return it after washing.

Now that a home has been provided, the subject of food is next on the list. Try to determine what the bird eats in its normal state. This is usually an easy task once you have identified the bird as to species. Generally, birds with strong, conical beaks are seed eaters, while those with slender, pointed beaks eat insects. A hooked beak signifies a raptor, or flesh-eating bird, while the strong, straight bill—such as that of the crow, jay or robin—indicates that a variety of foods may be eaten.

Seed-eating birds can be fed canary or parakeet seed, along with cracked sunflower seed. Add occasional greens such as bits of spinach, celery tops or the leaves and blossoms of clover. At first, some food should be placed in a dish, while more is scattered on the sand. Eventually, for cleanliness, you can put it all in the dish.

Sometimes if a few canary seeds are germinated on wet paper toweling in a covered dish, the resultant sprouts will tempt a bird when other foods fail. This ruse may be tried on insect eaters and general feeders, as well. Natural weed heads and tops of grass may also help finicky appetites, as will split cranberries, raisins and grapes. A bit of fruit should be provided for all birds to act as a laxative and help balance their diet.

General feeders should have a mixed diet. Earthworms, insects, mealworms, fruit and greens should be provided. The bird will balance its own diet if enough variety is available.

Remembering the Slice of Life, be sure to give your star boarder plenty of sunshine—but, as always, there should be available shade. If a screened porch or spare room is handy, the bird may take the opportunity to exercise. Cover surfaces against the droppings, and don't despair if a few messes occur. Just allow them to dry and they will brush up easily. After all, the bird that is generous with its waste is obviously processing its food, and that is a good sign. In nature, of course, a bird scatters its droppings as it goes; it has been recyling vital materials long before it became popular to do so.

Flesh eaters should have the meat-fur-feathers diet. As with all adult birds, they need fresh drinking water. When a bird is well enough to leave its enclosure and hop about the porch or room it should be provided with a shallow pan of water for a bath. The pan should be lined with wood, screening or cardboard so the bird will not lose its footing.

If you must keep your invalid in a cage, have the cage shielded on three sides to give the bird a feeling of security. And place it at eye level. Then, as you approach, you will not appear the overwhelming giant you might seem to be if the cage were on a low bench or table.

A caged bird is an open invitation to cats and dogs. It is astounding what a determined cat can do. A friend of mine planned to surprise her daughter with a parakeet for Christmas, so she hid the bird beforehand, in a neighbor's house. Because the neighbors had a cat, the caged parakeet was hung from a ceiling lighting fixture, well above eye level and in the center of the room. Then, feeling that the bird was secure, the family retired for the night.

In the morning they discovered their mistake. The cage was still in place, but the bars had been ripped open and the unfortunate bird, of course, was gone. The cat had climped to the top of a chair, leaped to the cage, and clung there while it pulled the wires apart and demolished the bird.

Barring such unfortunate attacks, however, the day may come when all your efforts bear fruit. You remove the splint, trim off the bandage, and open the door to freedom. If you have cautiously refrained from handling the bird any more than necessary, during its convalescence it will be still wild and ready for its release. It will dart out into the sunshine without a pause and be gone so quickly that you will have no time to click the camera and record its flight.

The bird that is fouled by an oil slick may be beyond your help. Often the oil is bunker oil from a ship —thick, black and gluey. Unable to swim because of its matted feathers, the bird flounders to shore. When you find it, it is cold and exhausted. Most likely it has swallowed some of the oil in an attempt to preen its feathers.

The best thing to do, in such a case, is to quiet the bird with a gentle hood. Place a wrap of cloth around it to keep it from struggling further. Provide warmth as soon as possible: room temperature or better. This will comfort the bird and make the oil easier to work with.

If the bird is only lightly soiled, remove the oil with sawdust or Fuller's earth, available at drug stores. Heavier doses of oil may be removed by *careful* sponging with a detergent. But don't soak with the detergent because that will burn the bird's tender skin and remove its natural feather oils.

If the condition is hopeless, the most humane step is to put the bird to sleep. A few drops of chloroform on a wad of cotton placed over the unfortunate creature's nostrils will bring a painless death.

If the bird is in somewhat better condition, you may be able to keep it in a pen with access to drinking water. It will preen its feathers constantly, gradually restoring their natural oil.

Feed the bird with a game-bird mixture, if available. Many aquatic birds must muddle their food in water before they can swallow it. A moistened mixture of dog food, minced clams and baby cereals can be given those birds that normally feed on animal material. Dabbling ducks, such as blacks, mallards and teal may have chicken mash and grain.

When normal feather condition has returned, release the bird as soon as possible. We once had a loon that had become oil soaked; I cleaned it and kept it in Peg's bathtub, feeding it on smelt and small fish from a local bait store. Two weeks later I returned it to the water, suitably cleaned and apparently fully recovered. Peg, on her part, went back to clean up a mammoth bathtub ring.

One more bird in the hand before we finish. This is the chick or duckling that often greets an ecstatic child on Easter morning. Although the traffic in new-hatched fowl has been outlawed in many places, baby chicks and ducks and geese are still surreptitiously hatched, sold and received—often literally—with

133

open arms. And small wonder that the underground trade continues—fluffy little hatchlings are lovable tykes.

But that's one of their troubles: they are too lovable. There is the uncontrollable desire to pick them up and cuddle them to your cheek. If the chick is allowed to stand on your hand and then gently lifted, that is one thing. But by grasping it in your hand you will bend those pliable bones. And for two children who quarrel over who gets to hold little Chirp—that is another story. Chirp may be injured for life by those who love him best.

If the chick survives the excitement, he may yet have a chance—that is, while you look for a poultryman who will take him. Few families can cope for more than a week or two with a growing chicken or a burgeoning duck. But while he is yours, your first concern is to give him a comfortable home.

With little Chirp, as with any baby bird, warmth is essential. A cardboard carton with a 40-watt bulb overhead for heat will make a comforable home. Place a thermometer at the same level as the chick; he should bask in a temperature of 85 degrees or better, with a shelter so he can escape the heat if needed.

Provide fresh water in a dish so placed that he cannot step in it or soil it with his droppings. Sprinkle coarse sand on the floor of the carton; this will serve as absorbent litter and will supply the gravel he needs for proper digestion. His food should be chick starter mash obtainable at a pet store, moistened enough with water to be crumbly. Or if the store cannot supply the mash, you can feed him Pablum or baby cereal, slightly dampened with a little water. Keep food constantly available.

The same diet can be used for ducklings or goslings. A few sprouted grains and "chick feed"—finely cracked corn often sold for feeding wild birds—can also be added. These web-footed waddlers will appreciate enough water to wade in, but you will have to change their litter more frequently.

You can tell when things are going right for your small visitor. The sounds he makes will be contented little sounds—quite different from the insistent clamor he will set up when he is cold or hungry. If he sleeps right beneath the bulb, perhaps a little more heat is needed. If he sleeps as far away as possible, maybe he needs a little less. His droppings should be soft but not loose; the more greenery you give, the looser they become. If fecal material is caked around the vent, trim the downy feathers away with scissors, or soften the caked material with a cotton swab dipped in mineral oil.

Your pet will grow to maturity there in your twentieth floor apartment if you let him. Remember to pick him up by letting him stand on your hands. And if "he" turns out to be "she"—as happened in Rahway, New Jersey, to a pet who came to stay with some friends of mine—she may even lay an egg a day, commencing at about nine months of age.

My Jersey friends at least had a tiny backyard for Chanticleer—renamed Clarissa after her sex became apparent. But a duck or a goose, with its need for a puddle, would have been too much for almost any animal lover.

Sooner or later the day comes when you and that Easter gift must part company. You get in touch with the county extension agent or the local SPCA until at last, you find someone who will take your pet. Then you trundle him off to his new home.

When you return, that box is strangely forlorn. The food dish, so important just an hour ago, is now just a funny container with a few morsels of grain. Things are quiet, empty.

It is the same when you release any bird. Suddenly

135

you realize that more than the cage is empty. But that is the way of a bird, and that is its very essense: it is as much spirit as it is flesh.

And that is why, to turn the phrase around the other way, a bird in the bush is worth two in the hand.

10. ...And Two in the Bush

When the car in front of you slams on its brakes for no apparent reason, don't let it bother you. Just take quick evasive action and peer at the occupants as you pass. If they are craning their collective necks while the car windows are hastily lowered, they are your brothers under the skin. These people belong to the largest unofficial organization in the world—The Society of Bird-watchers, sometimes known to the drivers behind them as S.O.B.'s.

They are your brothers under the skin, also, of course, from the very fact that you are reading this book. Nowhere is the interest in animals more widespread than in "the observation of the activities of our avifauna," to quote from the matter-of-fact description of my most enjoyable college course: Professor

Manter's ornithology lab and lectures at the University of Connecticut.

There are an estimated ten million structures for wild birds hanging from trees, stuck on posts and tacked to windowsills all over the United States and Canada. If each one serves an average family of four humans—plus, of course, all those birds—there are forty million people occupied in bird-watching in North America. Add to these at least an equal number who are interested but do not put out feeders or nest boxes, and you are approaching the hundred million mark. It's hard to get even rough estimates of exact numbers for, like the driver who brakes, swerves and gawks at a feathered flash on the landscape, a person can become a bird-watcher on a split second's notice.

Perhaps I'd better dwell on that word "bird-watcher" for a moment. The more official segments of the birding public would like to see the word drummed out of existence. It suggests passive interest, they say, like plunking yourself down in front of the tube with your favorite beverage and a bunch of calories you don't need. And bird watchers—or, to use the more proper term, birders—are anything but passive.

Accompany the members of our Forest and Field Club of the National Audubon Society's Christmas bird count, for instance. There we stand, on the shores of Lake Champlain at eight degrees above zero, staring into the teeth of a gale that whips the spray onto the bushes like rime ice on a polar ship. Peg and I wipe the tears from our eyes while Cassius and Bea Guyett solemnly confer between themselves in total dedication to the task at hand.

"I dunno," says Cassius. "I make it seventy Canada geese, but sometimes it seems like seventy-one. How many do you get, Bea?"

Bea squints through the scope, and comes up with a

different figure. Then they turn to us. "How many did you and Peg get, Ron?"

I dutifully bend my own telescope and blink at the honkers. They sit out there in the chop as unconcerned as if it were a balmy day in June. I lose count somewhere around eleven. So, after a suitable pause, I finally straighten up, saying nothing. Perhaps Peg will announce the results of her count, but she is playing it cool, too—in more ways than one.

"I didn't quite get the total," I finally confess. "But I'd say we were safe at seventy."

Such antics go on from dawn till dusk all over the country sometime between mid-December and New Year's Eve. There are guesstimates ("probably fifty evening grosbeaks at the top of that old tree, wouldn't you say, Peg?") and excited single sightings ("we walked half a mile through snow up to our knees, but it was worth it. The bald eagle was perched in his old tree on Long Point, just like last year!").

At the supper table we add up the day's count. Last Christmas we tallied fifty-five species. We also add up the miles we walk, the miles we ride, and the total number of hours in the field. Paying our dollar to the National Audubon Society for the privilege of frozen fingers and frostbitten eyeballs, we leave those fifty-five species somewhere out there in the dark and crawl wearily into bed.

Active, yes—no matter what we call ourselves, you and I, and one out of every four Americans. Or at least we can be. Bird-watching—or birding—can involve rappelling down a cliff to take a photograph of a falcon's nest. It can get you up before dawn and keep you out after midnight. It can even get you shot, as happened a century ago to those heroic persons who first tried to prevent the killing of breeding egrets for their "aigrette" plume feathers. But today birding is the most popular spectator sport on our continent.

139

That branch of birding that involves the feeder and the nest box is ideal for our purpose. It puts the wild pets exactly where they should be—free to come and go as they please, but close enough so you can enjoy them. Although they were not thrust on you like the salamander brought home from camp or the baby skunk who wailed with hunger and cold, these several million "pet" wild birds should receive some attention in these pages.

Man-made nest boxes and feeders are vital to today's birds. They help supply, in neat packages, the two basic requirements of any species for food and shelter. It's indeed fortunate that we can provide these necessities, for birds have suffered grievously at our hands. And the culprits are not only the hunters with their scatter guns, the egg collectors, and the men with poles who knock passenger pigeon squabs to earth where they burst like ripe melons. The plow, the bulldozer and the chainsaw have done away with brush, swamps and overgrown land—prime territory for wild birds.

One of our most beloved of birds, the bluebird, is being done in by the very person who appreciates him most—the farmer, who looks forward to the bluebird's warbling song as it arrives every year to resume its war on insect pests. But the farmer, in his efforts to use every last square foot of land and give the farm that well-kept look, cuts down the old trees and clears away the fence rows. Hardly a knothole is left for the bluebird to use for a nest. Even the knotty wooden fencepost, so long a part of picturesque rural America, is giving way to the sterile metal post with its single strand of electric wire. And the few available nesting holes are often taken over quickly by that raucous squatter, the European starling, or its fellow rowdy, the house sparrow.

Fortunately, something can be done to help the bluebird. It takes readily to nest boxes. It is not fussy, either, as to the height or type of box provided. I recall one spring when a male bluebird arrived to investigate the nests we have around the place. As luck had it, every birdhouse was occupied by tree swallows. Fearing that our visitor would search elsewhere, I hastily slapped together a few pieces of board for a box. Lacking a drill to make the required inch-and-a-half entrance, I roughed out a square hole of the approximate size with a small keyhole saw.

Tacking the box to a handy fencepost, I quickly retired to the house. The whole procedure took no more than fifteen minutes. That bluebird must have been watching because he was actually at his door before I had returned to mine. He took possession at once, inveigled a female to toss in with him, and together they hauled a handful of hay and grass to that inelegant abode. Then, although I marveled that the hasty carpentry held together long enough, they presented four flourishing young'uns to a waiting world.

There are many good books that give exact dimensions of bird boxes, size of entrance hole and other vital statistics. However, the gradations in size, slope of roof and color scheme are, I believe, completely lost on their occupants. A bird needs a shelter for its young, away from the presence of other members of its same kind, and reasonably free from danger of enemies. If it is a hole-nesting species it needs an entrance large enough to admit its body, plus a cavity sizeable enough for the sitting female. The birds themselves seem to care little whether the box faces north or south or whether it's built of aromatic cedar or equally aromatic tarpaper.

This is not to say that birdhouses should be constructed with no regard for their expected tenants. In spite of those birds that have built homes in the pockets of old jackets, on the window ledges of posh seaside villas or—like Suzie the duck in Lodi, Wisconsin, on a

141

railroad bridge so trains have to be rerouted—there are still some basic suggestions to follow.

Among the requirements for a successful nest box are those of comfort and safety, both for the parents and the young. A knothole in a tree is usually shaded part of the day, but your nest box is out in the open. Ventilation in the form of some small openings near the roof can be most important. A sloping roof is better than a flat one as it will help shed rain. But drill holes in the floor of the box, anyway, so unwanted water can drain away.

Wood for nest-box construction should be inch-thick boards, rough on at least one side. The front panel with the entrance hole should be placed with the rough side inwards, for the young birds to cling to as they climb out. The hole itself should match the size of the bird, and should be about a third of the way down from the top.

As to external ornamentation and color, here's that Slice of Life again. A peg at the entrance hole may satisfy your need for a threshold, but it probably doesn't matter to the bird. Very few treeholes come complete with doorstep. And with regard to color, the most natural shade is deadwood brown. You may stain the boards, if desired, or even paint them. But, again, the choice is up to you. However, it helps to paint the roof white, and not merely for esthetic reasons. White paint deflects the sun's rays and gives a cooler house.

Direction of exposure can vary, too. We have fifteen bird boxes ranged in a circle around our home, all facing the house so we can get a good look with binoculars or telephoto lens. All fifteen are occupied each year. Not all natural treeholes face conveniently south, supposedly the proper exposure for the well-bred bird. The main reason to erect your birdhouse one way or another might be so you could observe it

142

easily, or turn it away from the prevailing direction of storms.

The size of the cavity can also be variable. Although woodpeckers, chickadees and nuthatches will enlarge a cavity in pulpy wood if it is too small, the general bird populace usually must take things as it finds them. For most purposes, actual inside dimensions of five by five inches, with a height of ten inches, will be large enough to accommodate bluebirds, tree swallows, chickadees, titmice and nuthatches. The purple martin, which is a large, sociable swallow, may have a colony box of six-by-six-by-six-inch compartments (inside measurements) with a two-and-a-half-inch hole for each compartment.

Wrens can nest in a four-by-four-by-six-inch high space, but these effervescent little birds will actually accommodate themselves to anything that suits their fancy. Certainly they will not balk at spacious or unusual quarters; my grandfather had to give up his barn boots for one summer because a pair of house wrens had remodeled the left one.

House wrens, by the way, can be both the joy and the despair of the bird box set. The male bubbles with energy and song, but his enthusiasm may boil over. In an apparent effort to give the female a choice, he may fill half a dozen nest boxes with twigs —even if those boxes are already occupied. He will put a few twigs in a hole while the rightful parents are away, thus discouraging them from further visits. Then he finishes the job, sometimes packing three inches of twigs right on top of the other couple's helpless young. To make things worse, his mate may not choose that box at all, so the young have died for nothing.

The wren is smaller than most of its neighbors, so a small entrance hole will not discourage it. However, a much more serious interloper can be eliminated by careful attention to dimensions. This unwelcome visitor is the European starling. An undersized starling can barely squeeze through the one-and-a-half-inch standard bluebird hole in a thin board, but usually finds the tunnel effect of an inch-thick board too tight for comfort. But, in deference to my friend in Norman, Oklahoma, who will probably never see a bluebird or swallow or titmouse there in the middle of the city, the size of entrance hole for starlings is two inches.

House sparrows—or English sparrows, to use their other name—will also build in nest boxes. Perhaps you want them, perhaps you don't. But, given their choice, they seem to prefer holes quite high in the air. Bluebirds, tree swallows and chickadees, on the other hand, will build at eye level. Thus a low box may discourage house sparrows.

A friend of ours, Les Jaquith, has such an unusual means of eliminating unwanted birds that I'll pass it along to you. He rigs up what he calls his Chamber of Horrors: a nest box with a trapdoor over the entrance. The trapdoor is hitched to a string, on the other end of which is Les at a window in the house. When the starling or house sparrow enters the box to investigate, Les pulls the string. The door shuts and latches, making the bird a prisoner.

Les leaves the door shut several hours, or even overnight. It is hard to tell what passes through the poor bird's brain, but when he is released in the morning he has had enough. Bursting from the box in full flight, he makes a beeline for the distant horizon. "And," Les grins, "we never see him again."

Other undesirables are brought by the birds themselves. Some birds are a veritable flying menagerie. They may bring with them feather lice, leg mites and assorted other passengers. When the bird family finally leaves, a number of these hangers-on may stay behind. So some means of cleaning the box must be provided. In addition, the remains of the last nest must be removed to provide for the next tenants. A hinged roof or side or bottom—with a secure latch so it won't fly open in a windstorm—will allow you to clean house, tossing out bugs and bedding in one motion. You can dust with pyrethrum powder if there's a chance that another family will be raised in the same house that season; otherwise, postpone cleaning until spring, when all those little guests will be gone, anyway.

While you're cleaning and making repairs, you may discover that the empty birdhouse hasn't been as empty as you thought. A whitefooted mouse may have moved in during the winter, adding his own furnishings of soft grasses and milkweed down. Cocoons and other insects, spiders and millipedes often make a winter birdhouse into a tiny, slumbering zoo. More than fifty species of insects have been reported from abandoned birdhouses, plus approximately the same number of species of snails, centipedes, sow bugs, spiders and other hibernators.

Last spring a friend of mine opened a birdhouse to clean it and quickly closed it again. It had become the abode of a family of soft-furred, large-eyed flying squirrels. Apparently he didn't frighten the gentle creatures enough to make them leave, and they remained into the summer—to the consternation of the tree swallows and house wrens that tried to set up housekeeping in that inviting box. So, in emptying birdhouses, better watch what you're hauling out and throwing away. Your cleanup chores may not be as routine as you expected.

We salvage some of the material to use again. The material consists of a small handful of white feathers from each tree swallow box. Tree swallows are practically addicted to white feathers. Each spring, as these graceful birds are getting ready to nest, we release a few of the feathers, one at a time, on the breeze. Scarcely has a feather ridden off on the wind than it is seized by a swallow. High into the air goes the swallow, dropping the feather and catching it again. Soon more swallows join the play, and the feather passes from one to the other until finally it is whisked into a box. If we release several feathers at once the air seems to be filled with giant snowflakes.

Feathers, no matter what their color, make good nest material for other birds as well. Bits of facial tissue are quickly used, and once I saw a barn swallow flying to its nest triumphantly trailing about six squares of toilet tissue.

The preference of birds for string is well known, so you can put some out for their use. But cut it in lengths of six inches or less. A bird can hang itself if the string gets tangled. A boy in Ferrisburg, Vermont lost his kite and the cord settled high in the top of a sugar maple tree. A starling picked up the cord and flew off, probably intending to use it for its nest. That was two years ago, and both cord and starling are still there. The bird got fatally twisted in the string. The tragedy became known when the leaves fell off the tree in the autumn.

Use care in setting up the birdhouse. There should be some means of protection from marauding animals. Cats, dogs and squirrels can be a menace to nesting birds. Even chipmunks can destroy a nest. In fact, our own small Munk, whom we raised on an eyedropper, thoroughly scrambled the three eggs of a tree swallow. So, where such perils threaten, you can stall off tragedy by providing a "cat guard"— a downpointing cone of metal extending at least eight inches out from the post and fixed five feet off the ground. And be sure the box is located where intruders cannot jump at it from some nearby elevation.

Then, too—although this amounts practically to heresy to many cat lovers who feel that Tabby has an inherent right to prowl the countryside—a cat can be controlled. This is especially important during May and June, when adult birds are nesting and the young are learning to fly. One woman brought two dying sparrow fledglings to me; she had taken them from her cat and had driven remorsefully more than forty miles in hopes I could save them. Her remorse changed to indignation, however, when I suggested that she confine Mittens or put him on a leash until at least the Fourth of July, when most birds would be able to take care of themselves.

And thinking of that Slice of Life again, it does little good to put a bell around a cat's neck. The sound of a bell means nothing in the normal experience of a bird. And a sudden tinkle as a cat springs is pretty late warning—even if the bird understood what the bell was for.

Safety should be considered in the location of a feeder, as well. Birds need plenty of visibility, especially when they are eating. A feeder next to a dense evergreen may be protected from the wind, but it also supplies a hiding place for potential enemies. Put the feeder a few feet out in the open; it may not be your idea of coziness, but it gives the birds a margin of safety in case of attack. With plenty of food they can keep active and warm, no matter what the weather.

Your feeding operation can be as simple as a few crumbs tossed out on the snow or a piece of beef fat hanging from a string. The best fat is known as suet; it's that hard fat found around the kidneys. You can put out other fat as well. A friend of mine spreads peanut butter on the bark of trees as if she were dabbing it on crackers. She mixes the peanut butter with bird seed to make it more crumbly and keep it from clinging to the bird's palate in an annoying mass.

Commercial birdfeed mixtures contain a number of seeds in various proportions: millet, hemp, milo, buckwheat, wheat and sunflower seeds, among others. Most finches, cardinals and sparrows will take any of these grains, while chickadees, nuthatches and titmice prefer the sunflower seed. Grosbeaks and crossbills know a good thing when they find it, too. They have learned to supplement their diet of tree buds and pine seeds with the sunflower seeds scattered in dooryards and feeders from their northern Canadian haunts clear down into South America—if any of them should ever happen to go that far.

Although suet and sunflower seeds are the staples that together will attract almost any winter bird, there are a number of other foods you can put out for variety. Finely cracked corn may be taken by the seed-eaters, while the more coarsely cracked kernels are relished by jays. Slices of orange and other fruit provide a change. And try hanging a doughnut from a string; it will be kept bobbing all day long as the chickadees and titmice work on it until 'it's just "a hole hanging in the air," as a small correspondent wrote to me.

Foods hung from a string, by the way, will swing precariously when sizeable birds such as jays and starlings try to alight on them. Smaller birds do not seem to mind the wild gyrations as much. A chickadee will alight on a doughnut, sending it spinning in, say, a clockwise rotation. Then another chickadee may alight on the same doughnut, whirling it in the other direction. No matter; these surefooted little birds are at home rightside up, upside down—or spinning at eighty revolutions per minute.

Less acrobatic birds may prefer their food presented in a more sedate manner. Juncos, goldfinches and pigeons commonly eat on the ground. Any of them can fly up to a feeder however—in spite of a bird book on my shelves that solemnly promises you'll not be bothered with pigeons if you have your feeder at eye level or above. A friend of mine, Mrs. Pat Harman, shoos pigeons away hourly from her windowsill feeder, some twelve feet above eye level. And thousands of pigeons get daily handouts on fire escapes and apartment window boxes.

To prevent the larger birds from eating a whole winter's supply by January, you can put a raised turkey-wire screen over the feeder. Turkey wire is one-by-two-inch rectangular mesh, and is sold in hardware stores. Squeeze every other two sides together a bit with a pair of pliers, thus making the opening in the mesh slightly larger than an inch. This will admit most sparrows, nuthatches and chickadees, while keeping out the jays, starlings, pigeons—and the grosbeaks with their attractive plumage but alarming gastronomic capacities. Sunflower seeds inside the mesh, mixed seeds and crumbs outside; it works out economically all around.

There is one other item of food that should be mentioned. That item is the birds themselves. A concentration of half a hundred birds represents a bonanza for a winter hawk or shrike. Every year we are visited once or twice by one of these birds on its rounds over the countryside. The potential victims "freeze" if they spot their enemy in time, or scatter wildly if it careens down on them from behind a local evergreen.

The shrike is about the size of a robin; it captures its prey by overtaking it in flight and battering it to earth. So the smaller birds flee to the shelter of the syringa bush. There they creep into the tangle of branches in its center. The shrike follows them as best it can, and an eerie chase ensues. We watch as perhaps a dozen chickadees and sparrows climb through the branches like mice, while the shrike shoulders its way after them in an attempt to force one out into open flight.

Usually the contest ends in a draw, with all the birds on one side of the bush and the frustrated shrike on the other. But, occasionally, a bird is crippled and slow to flee, or for some reason it lacks the alertness that characterizes most songbirds. This bird instantly becomes the target of the predator. In a few seconds it is all over. Then the remaining birds go back to their feeding, their whole race strengthened by the elimination of the weakling from their midst.

This little drama, by the way, illustrates what is known as the "sanitary value" of predators—a concept recognized unconsciously by woodsmen for years, but only recently applied to flesh-eaters by a penitent mankind attempting to raise predators from the lowly status of "varmints." Just like plants in a garden, the ranks of wildlife are better for pruning and thinning and weeding.

There is one danger that may strike all your wild pets at once. Remember that they become dependent on the daily provision of food. And if you should go away for a long weekend, or some crisis makes you forget to feed them, the birds may suffer. If you leave home for a period, be sure the birds are adequately cared for in your absence. It's better not to start feeding them at all than to desert them when the snow is deep and the cold is bitter—which is when many otherwise thoughtful people shut up the feeder and head south.

There is no reason, by the way, not to feed the birds all year round. They will visit your feeder, only less frequently, all summer. A handful of inert seeds and a chunk of fat languishing in the heat cannot compare with the lure of delicious insects and sunripened fruit. But as the young take to the wing, the busy parents

151

will welcome the easy pickings at the feeder to help satisfy those clamoring mouths. Each year we watch as overgrown adolescent woodpeckers, chickadees, nuthatches and purple finches follow their parents from tree branch to feeder and back again.

There's another advantage to summer feeding. You'll attract birds more richly attired than the somewhat somber-hued winter species. Orioles and tanagers will feed on raisins and orange slices. Catbirds will carry on a running battle with the hairy woodpeckers for the suet. Rose-breasted grosbeaks will shell out the sunflower seeds as fast as their winter relatives, but since they are not so clannish as the pine or evening grosbeaks, there are fewer of them. And there will be some birds around your yard that will not use the feeder at all, but will linger because of the mere presence of other species.

In winter you may have had eight woodpeckers and half a dozen cardinals. But in the summer their ranks are thinned down. You may see only one or two of each species. This is because of the strong territorial instinct of nesting birds. Except for sociable types like house sparrows and purple martins, few birds will tolerate the presence of others of their kind during the breeding season. A robin will accept a pair of song sparrows, say, or a brace of flickers, but no other robins—at least, not closer than two or three hundred feet.

It is well to remember this need for elbow room as you put out bird boxes. Peg and I can have fifteen occupied birdhouses around our home because they are arrayed in a huge circle five hundred feet in diameter. But only one or two of those birdhouses would be in use at one time if they were all crammed into a small back yard. The same is true of nesting platforms—eight-inch squares of board put up under the eaves of a house for use by phoebes, robins and barn swallows.

Platforms in all four corners of an open porch will not necessarily mean four bird families. It may mean only that one pair of birds has four choices.

Around a bird bath, however, many barriers are lowered—just as they may be lowered at a tropical water hole, where lion and gazelle occasionally drink only a few feet apart. A bird bath may have regular visitors that come from a quarter of a mile away. The bath should be wide and shallow, with a roughened bottom so the birds can keep their balance while splashing water over themselves.

Apparently the bath has some therapeutic value, like a medicinal hot springs. A canary in its cage may take a bath with only a few drops of water at a time, dipping its beak in the drinking cup and going through the motions as if it were standing in a fountain. And one time Peg called me to the window to watch a purple grackle having the time of its life under a downspout in the middle of a rainstorm.

Most of the suggestions thus far have been in the nature of providing man-made devices to appeal to the birds. But here, as with practically no other group of living creatures, you can provide natural attractions as well. If your own home is limited in landscape possibilities, there may be a local park—or even a vacant lot—in which you can try your hand. Usually it is easy to get permission to tinker with the greenery, as plants that attract birds are often pleasing to the eye.

A park or vacant lot whose trees and shrubs lose their leaves in autumn may be alive with birds in summer but almost deserted in winter. A few scattered evergreens will cut down on the starkness and may help the birds utilize wild foods that are already there. One famous study along these lines showed that a covey of bobwhite quail actually starved to death in the base of a haystack rather than seek food in a

153

nearby open cornfield that was hunted over by a hawk.

The "hawk" doesn't necessarily have to be real; there could merely be a potentially dangerous situation where songbirds would simply not take chances. A few well-placed evergreens could change all that. They would act as escape cover, provide shelter from the wind and make a more interesting landscape.

As for food plants, the formula is really quite simple. A plant that produces fruit is potential bird food. This is true whether the "fruit" is a nut, seed, berry, or something as prosaic as an apple. Many ornamental shrubs are especially good for food. The common service berry (*Amelanchier*), sold in nurseries as "Sarvis tree," has abundant white blossoms in spring, with deep red blueberry-shaped fruit in summer. Flowering plum, crabapple and hawthorn look good in spring to us, and taste good in winter to the birds. When I was studying the food habits of the bobwhite quail, I discovered that a regular item of its diet was the fruit of the flowering dogwood, one of the most spectacular spring trees.

The fall fruits of hackberry, autumn olive and choke-cherry make good early winter feeding. Box-elder or ashleaf maple holds its winged fruit all winter, and will attract seed-eating birds until spring. And one of the best trees of all is the mulberry. But if you put it in a public park, don't let anyone know you planted it. Those squashy berries create one awful mess, even though they may attract as many as half a hundred recorded species of birds.

Or put in a few flowers. Hibiscus, nicotiana, trumpetvine, hollyhock, fuchsia and honeysuckle will be visited by hummingbirds while in flower and by seedeating birds when mature.

Whether your flair is for gardening, landscaping, carpentry, photography or sculpting birdbaths, you'll find something to occupy you while you satisfy your interest in bird-watching—excuse me, birding. You can eat your cake and have it, too: caring for a flock of pets while they remain free.

You can even get in your car and screech to a halt while you peer at a silhouette in a tree, oblivious to the car behind you.

And, by the way, if you happen to be the driver of Car No. 2, be careful of Car No. 1. Blow your horn, yes. Screech on the brakes. Take clever evasive action. Glare at him as you pull out and around him. Shout four-letter words.

But please do not hit him. After all, that bird-watcher might just happen to be me.

11. Fur Coats and Warm Milk

There's an old chunk of material in the garage that is one of our most valuable aids in the care of orphaned mammals. I paid 25 cents for it years ago at a rummage sale. Since then it has helped in the rescue of numbers of young wild creatures: raccoons, skunks, woodchucks, squirrels, rabbits, opossums, mice and porcupines, to name a few.

My lucky purchase was an old fox fur. Sometime in the past a red fox had been killed and skinned, and the pelt made into the collar of a coat. After having graced the throat of one—or perhaps many—ladies, the fur was finally separated from the coat. It wound up on the bargain table at the annual Ladies Aid rummage sale, considered and rejected by dozens of potential buyers until I came along and bought it for a quarter.

When we are faced with some woodland foundling, down on his luck and starving, we dig out the fox fur. It is tattered, and has long been in two pieces, but it still retains a bit of its lustrous sheen. And it is still capable of quieting the chattering teeth, calming the jittery nerves and warming the shivering body of some unfortunate who has been placed in our care.

While Peg uses her motherly touch and tone on the waif, I get out a piece of the fox fur. Then I find one of various cages or boxes suitable to the size of our small visitor. Mice and chipmunks can use a shoebox, or even a berry basket, together with the smaller piece of fur. Young rabbits will fit in a cardboard carton. And the larger animals, together with the larger chunk of fur, go into one of several wooden cages we have fashioned for our animal hospital.

Two orphaned foxes we had, naturally, were right at home in the fur. But so have been the other young mammals, for even a rabbit does not seem to recognize an enemy until it has had a brush with death. Besides, it has been years since that pelt raced over the landscape and all canine smell is gone. The orphan is aware only that the fur is comforting and soft like its mother. We place a heating pad beneath the box and perhaps a ticking clock nearby to perk up the orphan's interest in life.

With the warmth soaking through its body the youngster is now ready for a meal. We usually assume it to be hungry, as there have doubtless been many hours, or days, since it was fed. But until warmth and comfort are supplied, the small digestive system may not be working. A chilly young mammal may choke on the same mouthful of food it would swallow eagerly when more at ease.

The standard diet for these young animals is the

same as for human babies: warm milk. But ordinary cow's milk is too rich for many tiny stomachs. Peg and I put two parts of whole milk to one part of water. Then we add honey at the rate of a teaspoon per cup of the mixture, plus a quick dash of salt. Most animals have a sweet tooth, we have discovered. They will usually eat salt when they can get it, too, so the concoction may appeal to their taste buds. Besides, these additives supply extra energy and minerals.

The milk should be heated slowly so it doesn't scorch. It should be fed at about body temperature, but it's better to have it too cool than to take a chance on burning those tiny innards.

Next step: transfer the food from the stove to the stomach—almost as simple as that. But not quite. There are a number of ways to feed a nursing mammal and most of them can be messy.

If the patient is a tiny creature, such as a mouse, even the slender tip of a medicine dropper is too large for that groping little mouth. We use a cotton swab on a stick, such as a Q-Tip. Dipping the swab in the milk, we try to ease it gently between those tender lips. If we're successful, fine. If not, we merely smear a little on the outside and wait. Soon a little pink tongue appears. It makes a quick swipe of the lips. We apply another coating of food and wait a second time. Usually, within ten minutes the little fellow is chewing on the swab as if he'd never let go. Although each swab holds only a drop or two, it takes only a few drops to fill that tiny stomach.

With squirrels, chipmunks, rabbits and animals of a similar size we use a medicine dropper. As with the mouse, if the food is not taken at once, we merely paint the outside of the mouth with warm milk, and let the natural licking reaction get things started. As soon as the animal associates the good taste on its lips with the touch of the medicine dropper, the feeding problem is solved. But to try to force food down its throat without letting the animal make its own discovery can be frustrating—to say nothing of getting the sticky milk everywhere but where it belongs.

With larger animals, such as infant raccoons, woodchucks, skunks and foxes, we use a plastic bottle. Occasionally a doll bottle is sturdy enough to be used, but many of them leak or collapse. The ordinary baby bottle has too large a nipple, and the flow of milk depends on the sucking reflex, which may be almost nonexistent in a young animal weakened by starvation. The ordinary ketchup squeeze bottle seems to work out best. With gentle pressure a supply of milk can be kept flowing, and the plastic tip is soft enough to be acceptable to those tender gums.

The amount fed at any given time will be determined by your small guest himself. When he's full, he'll stop. We fed our two orphan porcupines with a medicine dropper; as long as they were feeding contentedly they made murmuring sounds like a nursing baby. But when they had had enough the sounds became petulant little squeals. In case we were slow to get the message, they would knock the medicine dropper away with a round-house blow from one of their front paws, and chatter their teeth in agitation. Never once did they attempt to put things straight by sticking us with their quills. Afer all, we were Mother, and such tactics were only for enemies.

As with baby birds, many young mammals will eat only a bit at a time, but often. A rule of thumb is to try feeding at two-hour intervals. Normal eating habits depend on normal living conditions in the wild. A squirrel, whose mother is seldom far away, will nurse several times a day. A fawn, who must lie quietly in a woodland glade for many hours before its mother steals in for a visit, makes every meal a banquet. We had a tiny doe fawn, weighing about seven pounds, who would put away nearly a pint of milk at a feeding —about one-seventh of her weight.

The ultimate in feeding arrangements is that of the newborn opossum. Born at such an early stage that it looks like a little pink grub, the tiny creature claws its way to the mother's pouch. There it attaches itself to a teat so firmly that it is almost grafted onto her. Thus it receives an almost constant supply of nourishment until it is old enough to try a little variety in its meals.

If you have seen a dog feeding her puppies—or, for that matter, almost any animal nursing its young— you will note that the mother often licks the nether end of her offspring while it is feeding. This recalls Don Gill's statement that the food of a young animal goes straight through. The gentle moist action of the mother's tongue stimulates healthy bowel elimination. With a warm washcloth you can duplicate the action, if necessary. At any rate, be prepared for the end result of the intake of food soon after feeding.

When the youngster gets older it will usually reserve a portion of its cage for the performance of bodily functions. Rabbits and some rodents, however, never seem to become housebroken—or cage broken. They will eliminate their fecal pellets all over the place. This, doubtless, is nature's way of spreading valuable waste materials indiscriminately and without favor.

Although the immediate crisis has been solved when a young animal is warm and feeding, new problems begin to appear. What kind of shelter should be provided? What are the choices for food when it's time to change from a milk diet? What adjustments should be made now so that the creature eventually can make its way back to the wild?

The answer to these questions is another question: what would be normal for an animal this age? If it is a squirrel, it would be climbing, so give it something to climb on. The same is true of a porcupine, or—to a lesser degree—a chipmunk. A piece of tree limb, with the rough bark still intact, provides exercise for those sharp little claws.

If it is a burrowing animal such as a skunk, woodchuck or badger, try to find some means to satisfy its burrowing instinct. Ideally this would be a plot of earth where it could dig all it wished. However, unless the wire of the cage goes well into the soil, your little miner will excavate his way to freedom before he's ready for all that responsibility. The alternative is a box of soil, or even a pile of old rags in a corner.

Woody, the woodchuck who was raised by a friend of ours, solved the burrowing problem all by himself. When he was tiny our friend, Mrs. Mary Marsh, kept a quart bottle of warm water in an old wool sock as Woody's "mother." As he grew, she removed the bottle but left the sock for companionship. In poking around, Woody discovered the opening of the sock. He nuzzled his way down to the toe, and from then on the old sock was his refuge. He'd come out to feed and to play until he had had enough. Then he'd find the opening of the sock and burrow his way back to the toe again. Even if Mrs. Marsh moved the sock all over her kitchen and garage, Woody would search it out and burrow in.

A pen should be made of wire, or at least lined with it, so animals cannot chew their way out. A rabbit pen, complete with wire bottom, can be moved around the lawn for a continuous supply of fresh greenery.

Nonburrowing, nonclimbing animals should also have contact with the soil, if possible. A little grass, a bit of forest humus, some sand or loam will serve as a preview of the day when the cage door will open for the last time and the animal will be on his own. Place the soil in a pan or shallow tray. Often you'll find that it will be used just as the domestic cat uses a tray of kitty litter, and cleanup chores will be simplified.

Kitty litter, by the way, makes a fine covering for the floor of the cage or box. It is odorless, absorbent and provides a nonskid surface that is superior to a smooth floor. You can also use wood chips, sawdust, straw or pine needles. Little toes and feet need an uneven surface for proper development.

No matter how playful and sociable a small animal may be, it should have a spot all its own for privacy. A smaller box within the larger one, or a partially closed-in corner, will be appreciated. Our friend, Mrs. Bessie Pixley, noted that I had neglected to provide a private place for a juvenile whitefooted mouse whose mother had been crushed when we were stacking some lumber. We had hastily put the mouse in a bare cage and had gone back to work on the lumber pile. So Bessie went to the kitchen, found a plastic cottage cheese container, cut a hole in its rim to serve as a door, and inverted it over the mouse.

The idea was an instant success. Up to that time he had been crawling around in the shredded newspapers on the cage floor, squeaking for the mother who would never come. Now he crept into his little igloo and remained quiet until we could find the time to care for him. We fed him milk for three or four days, weaned him on sunflower seeds, clover blossoms and berries, and released him right back in the lumber pile ten days later.

The process of weaning a small mammal is easier, I think, when its "mother" is only a piece of fox fur and a medicine dropper than when its real mother is present. The milk doesn't taste right, the teat is glassier than normal, and the schedule of feedings is dictated by such nonwild-mammal considerations as when the alarm clock rings, what's on TV and whether there's a long weekend coming up. So, usually, just leaving a dish with a wide choice of food may be all the weaning that is necessary. The young animal may pick out the proper items for itself.

For nibblers such as rodents, a shallow dish can be filled with sunflower seeds, unsalted nuts, bits of lettuce, kale and carrot, and a small cube or two of apple or other fruit. Keep experimenting until you find what goes best. A few hard nuts or a bit of bone should also be available for rodents and rabbits at all times. Their incisor teeth grow continuously throughout life, and must be kept worn down through constant gnawing.

A modern and helpful hand in feeding animals is provided by the use of pelleted foods. There are hamster pellets, rabbit pellets, even cattle and elephant pellets. These pellets are easy to obtain, do not spoil or create a mess, and are available at many pet stores. However, they should not be used to the exclusion of natural foods, since your main purpose is to raise the animal under conditions that will help it make its own way in the wild. So the closer an animal's diet comes to its normal menu, the better.

General feeders such as raccoons and skunks will appreciate fruit and vegetables, with variety in the form of bits of meat, earthworms and scraps of fish. The food, of course, should be kept fresh and not allowed to spoil. And don't bother taking the bones out of the fish. No such service is provided on the streambank. If you have ever examined the scats, or fecal pellets, of a raccoon or a skunk you would soon come to the conclusion that it must have a digestion like a cement mixer.

Even carnivores like the fox and wildcat can use variety in their diets. One of the indelible sights of my childhood was the view of a distant pasture where, day after day, we could watch a family of fox pups as they elaborately stalked and pounced on grasshoppers and crickets. In summer, when berries are

163

ripe, foxes may consume these delicacies almost to the exclusion of anything else. Wildcats will eat berries, too, and they will go crazy over catnip as any domestic tabby. The story of the fox and grapes is not all myth, either; the autumn scats of foxes may be composed almost wholly of grape seeds.

Somewhere in the process of weaning we remove that fox skin from the cage. It has done its job, serving as warmth and consolation, but a playful youngster could make short work of it. Just as a small raccoon will chew on a handy portion of its real mother, another raccoon may do the same to our long-suffering fur. So we place a piece of flannel in the nest for a few days to absorb the proper smell and atmosphere. Then, sometime when the foster-child is otherwise engaged, we spirit its "mother" out of the cage. After a few days' airing in the sun, the fur will be ready for the next waif.

With that security blanket of fur removed and with the diet expanded to include a number of chewables, the youngster is becoming more self-sufficient with each passing day. No longer is the box or small cage adequate for its use. Remembering that a wild animal exists without any physical fetters, the best cage now is one that has no bars or walls of any sort. However, this is seldom practicable because of roving dogs, cats, and errant automobiles. So the animal still has to be confined, at least for its own protection.

We have been lucky in having an old screened-in porch that has served as temporary quarters for many animals in this transitional period. There is a portion of an old tree nailed in one corner. Another corner has a large pan of sandy gravel; it has been used as a bathroom for several years by an assortment of animals. Although we change it frequently for sanitary reasons, enough of the aroma lingers on so the next animal quickly gets the idea as to what it is for. Two

nest boxes complete the furniture. One is about a foot square and the other is about the size of a small refrigerator.

There is also a shallow pan of drinking water. On occasions we have had muskrats and, in one instance, a baby beaver, complete with flat little wooden-spoon tail. Then we used a large pan. Muskrats, beaver and otter must have access to water to keep their delicate skin from drying and cracking. But their playful enthusiasm drenches everything in sight, so we put the whole works outside in a temporary enclosure.

Always, no matter what animal may be the current inhabitant, we provide one other ingredient: the continuous heat that seems so necessary to health. This warmth may be supplied in the form of a heat lamp, heating pad or even a gooseneck lamp, depending on the size of the animal and the general circumstances.

Heat may be a magnet to a young animal, even if he wears a fur coat. One time I found a juvenile muskrat on a country road, fully a mile from the nearest water. It was frightened and dusty and obviously alone in this threatening world. So I scooped it up and brought it home to release in a nearby marsh. We put it on the porch while I went to the garage to get some supplies, carelessly leaving the porch door ajar.

When I got back there was no muskrat to be seen. Quite obviously he had pushed the door open and had made his way into the house. Now he was hiding. But where? Even a little muskrat's teeth are sharp, and he's willing to use them. We all felt like climbing up on chairs until he was located.

Then my son, Roger, had an idea. Just like the little girl who found the horse by saying to herself, "where would I go if I was a horse and I went and he had," Roger ran through the same mental process—and came up with the muskrat. Almost as if he had hidden the animal there himself, he went to the refrigerator and gently eased it away from the wall. Down at the bottom was that little ball of fur, curled up next to the warm coils and the friendly, softly vibrating motor— sound asleep.

We got the muskrat back on the porch and set him up with a heat lamp, bits of apple and carrot, and a shallow pan of water. He stayed with us only a week. We had intended to take him to the marsh in a few days, but his adventuresome spirit got the best of us again. This time it was the front door of the porch that was not firmly closed. Doubtless he had listened long enough to the siren call of the river flowing fifty feet in front of his little black nose, and took the first opportunity to make his escape. He may be there yet, living in the river bank. Or, now that we realize that wanderlust is part of a muskrat's makeup, he may have gone straight out the door, across the river and over into the next county.

That porch door, by the way, is an essential part of our entire animal rescue program. After the animal has been on the porch a few days and is accustomed to eating and sleeping in certain spots, we take the next step. Except for the decision to try to raise the little fellow in the first place, this is the most momentous choice we have to make. It is the decision to leave the door open.

It sounds simple enough, but when you become attached to a creature, you tend to put off that day as long as possible. Of course, a great number of our wild foster children never make it into a cage or onto the porch if they are old enough to skip the milk stage. Instead, they spend their convalescence or adolescence in a convenient hollow tree or barn foundation, appearing daily for the handouts we provide. But for those creatures we have raised from a bottle or a medicine dropper this is a fateful day, indeed.

At last the time arrives. The food dish has been near the door for the past few days, and it is there now, ready to welcome the animal when he returns. He pokes his nose outside, and quickly draws back. Then he pokes it out again, this time following it with one tentative foot. Again the withdrawal. And so on, until he is a few feet from the door, sniffing at the grass and the marigolds and the gravel of the driveway.

From then on, he proceeds at his own speed. We leave the door open night and day, and keep the food and water dishes full. He may never come back. More often, however, he returns a number of times. But the returns are more and more infrequent until we see him no more.

It is hard to part with some creature you have raised from a frightened, helpless stray. And yet it must be, for a wild animal is at its finest only when it is allowed to remain wild. Letting it make its own way back to the wild is the best way to return it to its own. With a front yard of several hundred acres of woodland and river, our animal should suffer little from human interference. How it gets along with its wild neighbors is something we can only guess.

Occasionally we get a hint that our scheme may have worked. Gray squirrels are extremely rare in this mountainous section of Vermont, but not around our house. Every few weeks we see a gray; is it Sparky, or Lucifer, or Cleo? We don't know. And that raccoon asleep in the maple tree while the jays fairly burst with apoplexy screaming at it—could it be Scamper, coming back as close as she dares, just for old times' sake? Again, we don't know.

The most singular experience of all happened three years ago. Piney, the porcupine who was the star of my book, *How Do You Spank a Porcupine?*, had wandered away from our front porch on a balmy spring evening. He had been staying away for a day or so at a time, but at least he was gone for good. After a week of no porcupine, we closed the porch door and figured we had seen the last of him.

Then, more than a year later, Roger heard a noise on the back porch. Grabbing a flashlight, he shone it outside, and then raced upstairs to wake us. Quietly we stole downstairs and stood there at the back door, gazing at a dark blur on top of the porch pillar. We could hear a crunch! crunch! as shreds of wood were clipped out by powerful teeth.

Could it be Piney? I opened the door and spoke to him. Instantly the gnawing stopped. We shone the flashlight up at our bristly visitor, who brought all thirty thousand quills to full alert. Backing majestically down the pillar, he gathered his equilibrium for a moment and then made his way off into the darkness.

We cannot be sure that it was our porcupine, but it just could have been. The nearest porcupine woods are several hundred yards away. So it would have taken a certain singleness of purpose for a forest creature to cross open meadow to our house. But more important was the spot the cactus-critter had chosen when he arrived: that very porch pillar, the only one with a platform, on top of which Piney used to sit and gnaw as a youngster, nearly two years before.

Piney, by the way, spent a short time communing with the fox skin as a youngster. His predecessor, Pokey, who was orphaned in a forest fire, found an even bigger mother image in the form of Jack, our big old shepherd dog. Pokey, with quills carefully laid to rest, would curl up to Jack for as long as Jack would lie there. Sometimes he would climb on Jack's back and ride along like a jockey, with no apparent protest from the long-suffering canine.

On those rare occasions when a cat or dog serves as a foster parent, a number of problems are solved. The domestic pet provides warmth, friendship and protection for its unusual companion. The wildling may receive food as well, either directly if it is adopted by a nursing mother, or by sharing in the dish with the pups. Of course, there are occasional surprises, such as when the adopted "pup" goes scampering up a tree or burrows down into the ground and out of sight.

There are shocks, too, of another kind. Some friends of mine run a summer camp for boys and girls. Once they found a fawn that had fallen into a hole that had been dug for a flagpole. The fawn had broken its leg in an attempt to clamber out. After a veterinarian set its leg, "Hercules" became a camp mascot. He was adopted by Danny, the other camp mascot, a large Irish setter.

Things were fine all summer and autumn until Hercules, now almost full grown and feeling his antlers, decided the time had come to make a break for the woods. He picked out his route and fled—bowling poor Danny over as he went. When Danny tried to head him off, Hercules thumped him again. "A more dejected Irish setter we have never seen," wrote the Flynns in a letter afterward.

Probably the manner of parting was actually fortunate, for a grown buck can be a dangerous pet.

Full-grown wild animals are harder to care for than those taken in infancy. They have a distrust and fear that will never completely be overcome. This, for our purposes, is an advantage, for they will take more readily to the wild again. But it also makes them difficult to care for, as they may readily bite the hand that feeds them.

The less an adult wild animal is handled the better. If it is wounded, secure professional assistance. A veterinarian can anesthetize the animal while a bone is set or wounds are treated. Trying to repair damages on a conscious animal may cause more damage or even result in its dying of fright. Often the best way to promote healing is to leave a wound open; the animal's licking may be all the salve it needs.

Warmth may still be necessary, especially with an animal that is sick or has suffered a great deal. It's defenses are down, and it can easily lapse into pneumonia. Sometimes it will help to put an alarm clock close to it so the animal can hear the ticking. This may rouse its curiosity and keep its will to live high enough to pull it through.

Natural food is important, especially for a convalescent animal. But more readily available foods—puppy biscuits, canned dog food or vegetable trimmings from the supermarket—will do for short periods. Keep plenty of water available, too, and change the water daily.

These pages contain some of the thoughts taken from our experiences with wild animals. We have been lucky over the years in living on a large abandoned farm, with plenty of land. Sharing that land with native plants and animals has been our pleasure. Indeed, we regard it as a privilege, as we know that they were here first. Your horizons may not be as broad in point of acreage as ours, but as the hardbitten old Vermonter said when someone told him how landwealthy he was: "Maybe you're right, but you can't eat scenery."

So your "porcupine" may be only a squirrel hit by a taxi. And your convalescent ward may be only the back hall—when the landlord isn't looking. But perhaps, assisted by something we have said here, you can adapt our experience to your own situation. And to lessen suffering, even if it is of a squirrel that tangled with a taxi, can be a heartwarming feeling indeed.

Whether your charge is an adult or young animal, remember that you are its protector, not its owner. Legally it is the property of the state; biologically it belongs to the woods or fields. The sooner it can go where it belongs, the better.

Or, perhaps better still, don't start an animal hospital at all. Once you have the first one, to borrow that oldie about opening a bottle of olives, the rest will come easy. That is how we got started—with an injured skunk on Long Island—and its spiritual descendants have followed us clear up to Vermont.

At the moment, however, there seem to be no crises in the world of wild animals—at least none that have come to our attention. For three weeks, now, there has been not a single frantic phone call. No agitated stranger has knocked on our door with his elbow while he holds a Mysterious Box in his arms. So the fox skin lies, a mother forgotten by her children, in the corner of the garage.

But it is only a lull. As I type these words, it is winter and our last patient departed more than a week ago—a racoon with insomnia who went for a mid-winter stroll right into the path of an automobile. Come spring there doubtless will be another crop of orphans —or suspected orphans—chattering and wailing for attention.

Then out comes the fox skin again—in five pieces now, as it was torn asunder by a disgruntled young woodchuck last year.

Perhaps that skin has seen its last days. But a soft piece of flannel works about as well. And lucky it does; the bargain table at the annual rummage sale went up to a dollar last year.

Besides, there's nothing that fits into a fox skin quite as well as a fox.

12. Skunk in the Cellar

When Mrs. A. E. Hosley turned on her cellar light, she noticed a quick motion in the corner. Curious, she pulled away a couple of boxes for a better look—and fled back up the stairs.

Her visitor was a common striped skunk. There was no overpowering odor—yet. But such a situation was fraught with peril. So she telephoned the local police department.

"Nothing to it," the voice on the phone assured her. "Just make a trail of crumbs and bits of hamburger leading up the steps and out the hatchway door. The skunk'll follow the food and you can close the door when he's gone."

Relieved, she and her husband followed the directions. Scattering food behind them, they gingerly tiptoed through the cellar along the wall opposite the skunk's hiding place. Out the hatchway door they went, and onto the lawn. Then they retired to the house to await results.

As skunks are nocturnal, the scheme lay dormant until after nightfall. The next morning the Hosleys checked their results. The trail had worked perfectly.

Mr. Hosley called the police station. "How did the food trail work?" the dispatcher wanted to know.

"Fine," said Hosley. "Just great. Now we have *two* skunks in the cellar."

This experience is duplicated every year in thousands of homes. If it's not skunks, it's opossums, or bats in the attic.

Such occurrences are becoming more common as living space for man and animals commands a higher premium each year. Sometimes you encourage your unscheduled visitor; often you don't. The Hosleys' two basement tenants were in the latter category. On the other hand, the squirrel that pays a daily visit for the corn, sunflower seed and vegetable leftovers you put out for him is a more welcome creature.

One of my more unforgettable guests arrived late at night. It was the middle of winter, and I was sitting at the typewriter in my upstairs study, hammering out a magazine article. At my left elbow was the window with its windowsill bird feeder, just visible out beyond the glow of the desk lamp.

I had put birdseed in the feeder at dusk so there'd be food for the first visitors the following day. As I worked, I could hear the birds coming and going, shuffling through the seeds and scratching in the crumbly snow on the feeder.

Then, as the sounds penetrated my thoughts, something seemed out of place. What were birds doing at midnight on a bird feeder?

Carefully I turned my head. The noise hadn't been caused by birds at all. The birds were asleep, of course, and the night shift had taken over—a velvet-furred creature a little larger than a mouse, with large liquid-brown eyes and a long, soft tail.

My visitor was a northern flying squirrel. He had climbed the trunk of the big maple, forty feet away. Launching out into space he had spreadeagled, stretching the membrane between wrists and ankles, and glided to a landing on the feeder. So eagerly did he work at the sunflower seeds that I was able to raise the window and pose him for the flash camera merely by prodding him with my finger.

When he was finished, he turned and leaped soundlessly into the night. It was his only visit, at least that we knew of, and after he was gone it all seemed like a figment of my imagination. But when the pictures were developed, there he was among the seeds and snow crystals—a bit of the wild that had been shared with us for ten minutes.

In contrast, a visit that lasted two years occurred at the home of Stuart and Olga Huckins, in Duxbury, Massachusetts. Stuart was a forester and came to know wild animals as they really are: vital, dynamic creatures that are an essential part of the land. So, one spring night when Stuart went to put a bag of supper garbage in the container by the back driveway and discovered a skunk lingering nearby, he set the bag on the ground instead.

The skunk returned and sampled the garbage. Apparently it was favorably impressed, for it came back the next evening. More garbage was waiting for it, only this time nearer the house.

The visits became a nightly occurrence. Each plateful of food was served closer to the back door. Finally their guest was eating right off the welcome mat.

Then the skunk began to appear with a companion. The two of them would poke through the food on the doorstep, sometimes amicably, sometimes with a sudden spat over a choice morsel. "We weren't worried about accidents, however," Olga Huckins wrote us, "because skunks do not use their scent on each other."

One night, as they peered through the gloom, they thought they saw three skunks. Then, as they looked further, they saw another—and another. Five new skunks had arrived. They were young ones—frisky little kits, all showing color variations of the pattern of Skunk No. 1, who was obviously their mother.

Now there were seven skunks paying nightly visits. And this was only the start. Knowing the peaceful nature of the skunk, and encouraged by their friendliness, Stuart and Olga propped the door open and began feeding the skunks in the house. They coaxed them through the doorway and into the living room.

Nor was this all. As the months passed, more skunks arrived. The food supplies were increased accordingly. "By the second summer we were feeding sometimes as many as fourteen skunks on an evening, some on the porch and some in the living room," they wrote to me. "One night a raccoon followed the skunks into the living room and started a free-for-all. Believe me, we held our breath. But they solved the difficulty by themselves, and not one whiff of skunk!"

By this time the nightly parade through their home had become a local curiosity, and the Huckins' living room frequently had as many human as musteline visitors. They watched as Bushytail and Limpy tussled briefly over a piece of meat, while Bashful peeked through the doorway, apparently hoping that some scrap would fly in his direction. And the whole parti-colored party would melt respectfully aside at the

176

approach of Caesar, obviously the patriarch of them all, who ambled directly to any tidbit that suited him.

Finally I had the chance to visit the Huckins' home for myself. After supper my hosts prepared the nightly meal for their guests: table scraps, dog food, fig bars and chocolate cookies. At dusk we took our places in their well-appointed living room. I considered the fine furniture, the handsome rugs and draperies, the shelves with their wide assortment of books. Hardly the place you'd invite a skunk in for a visit—if you didn't know skunks. But Olga and Stuart knew there'd be no trouble.

And there wasn't. Only four skunks put in an appearance that night, but it was unforgettable: four wild, uncensored skunks running about over our feet and behind the chairs where Olga had hidden the food. Two of them even took cookies from my hand, their little warm black paws prying my fingers open for treats I held in a half-closed palm.

When we retired that night I recalled the words of a naturalist I had heard years ago:

"To label a mean, grasping man as a skunk is to slander one of God's most inoffensive creatures."

Few of us can have the good fortune of Olga and Stuart Huckins. But there are ways to encourage your own version of their skunks. Just as in attracting the birds, there's a chance to eat your cake and have it too: enjoying wild pets while they run free. Remembering the two necessities of food and shelter, you can view your own yard, or the nearest city park, or even a vacant lot as the potential counterpart of the Huckins' living room. Skunks and opossums, raccoons and rodents will reclaim their natural heritage if given half a chance.

Like the bird huddled in a bush while a hawk sits imperiously in a nearby tree, a wild mammal needs shelter from real and imagined enemies. Scattered

177

evergreens or, better still, an evergreen hedge to serve as an avenue from one area to another, may make both areas available where neither could be used by itself. Briar patches and thorn bushes serve as emergency refuges for today's small creatures just as they did for Br'er Rabbit in the day of Uncle Remus. Leave old trees standing; they will be hollowed out for nests by woodpeckers, and the abandoned woodpecker holes may be taken over by flying squirrels. It's a memorable sight to scratch on the bark of an old tree and see two or three inquisitive baby squirrels poke their heads out to see what caused the commotion below.

You can provide "bolt holes," too—places for a last minute dash just ahead of an enemy. A trench, one shovelful deep and covered over with a board except for the ends, will make a good escape shelter for rabbits, raccoons and opossums. Hollow logs or even old culverts will serve as well. Just one or two such shelters may mean the difference between having and not having small furry neighbors—no matter how tempting the food morsels you may put out for them. And the holes made by one species, such as a skunk or a woodchuck, are valuable for years as nesting and hiding places for many other animals.

Old lumber piles and brush heaps serve as shelter, too—and have an added advantage as sources of food. Many small animals and insects make their homes in lumber piles, thus serving as potential snacks for their larger neighbors. Brush heaps not only attract a variety of tasty creatures but when fresh are good eating themselves: rabbits and hares, mice, muskrats, beavers and deer may all nibble on the bark, young twigs and branches. Pile up the trimmings from hedges and ornamental shrubs, too; they'll be nipped shorter by mammals gratefully divesting them of their buds and bark.

If you saw a deer or a rabbit in a tree, you'd think your senses had left you, yet I have discovered rabbit-eaten blackberry canes higher than my head; Br'er Rabbit simply reached up and pulled them down to where he could nip off the ends. And deer often stand on their hind legs to sample overhanging branches. But usually such food is high in the air and out of reach, unless you come along and clip it down.

You can set out food plants for wild animals as well. Almost any fruit or seed will find some sort of taker when other food is scarce. My parents have a large flowering crabapple in their back yard in Connecticut. Its abundant fruit hangs on the tree all winter. The fruit is slowly eaten away by squirrels, opossums and an occasional raccoon, plus assorted birds. On a chunk of ground you may provide rose hips, sumac berries, birch and alder catkins, ash and maple keys, nuts of all kinds, persimmons, highbush cranberries and other viburnums, to name a few native species.

Even well-weathered apples, hanging on the tree until you'd think they'd be as palatable as a dishcloth, will be dug out from the snow after they have fallen. In fact, almost every animal will solemnly chew on a frozen apple, no matter how rotten it is. A teetotaling lady naturalist friend says it's because they like the crunchiness, but I also suspect that since apples turn to cider in their own jackets, the chance of a little glow on a frosty night figures in there somewhere, too.

Even such gummy, uninviting objects as pine cones can provide a meal for the right animal. Alternate freezing and thawing cause some evergreen cones to open and shut like venetian blinds, thus helping to release the seeds. A mouse may find a tightly closed cone too tough to tackle, but when the scales have loosened in the mild weather of late winter, the industrious creature can pull them apart. The stronger teeth of squirrels allow them to start on a pine cone whenever they find it, shucking off the scales in a veritable shower. Often the snow around some favored stump beneath a patch of evergreens may be inch-deep in pine scales where a squirrel has annihilated one cone after another. So coniferous trees may furnish food as well as shelter.

A dozen ears of dried corn and a few handfuls of fruit are good winter food. To this you may add a chunk of suet or a couple of bacon ends. Tucked into the end of a culvert or partly hidden at the base of a tree, they provide a bit of shelter, too. Like the birds, wild animals can withstand almost any weather if they have food to provide energy. So the shelter is as much against the sudden enemy as it is against the constant adversary of winter cold.

Ordinary salt makes fine flavoring for the winter meal. An old trick of trappers and hunters is to put out a salt lick to attract animals. It works just as well today even if you do all your shooting with a camera.

Place a beach umbrella or chicken-wire framework, suitably decked out with camouflaging branches and grass, where it will hide you and your camera. Put the salt on an old stump, with suet and birdseed nearby. Then you can "shoot" birds by day and mammals at night.

Incidentally, my Vermont neighbors sometimes put salt on an old stump they wish to eliminate. The chemical soaks down into the wood with every rain. Porcupines and other animals, in their quest for salt, will gnaw the stump right to the ground.

Since many mammals are nocturnal, you may often guess at the size of your animal population. But, given a chance, they may surprise you, both in numbers and variety. As many as three hundred meadow mice have been counted in an acre of lush grassland, although the ordinary maximum is less than a third that figure. A family of cottontail rabbits can exist on a plot of ground the size of a tennis court—about a quarter acre. So can a skunk and an opossum. All of these species, each eating different food, may live on the same plot of ground. Raccoons like a high hollow tree, if possible, but they will occasionally den up in a fallen log or jumble of rocks and join the other mammals in their after-dark wanderings.

You can find out what kinds of animals you have

by making a tracking station. This is easily done by watering a bare patch of soil near a food source until the surface is a flat layer of mud. Then, when the mud dries, it will take the impression of tiny feet: the childlike handprints and almost-human footprints of raccoon and opossum; the delicate two-and-two tracery of hopping rodents and rabbits with the hind feet planted first; inch-wide plowed furrows of inquisitive shrews, sniffing busily for any insect or other edible; perhaps even the pointed impression of a deer's cloven hoof. Tracks in the dust or snow are similar, but are apt to crumble and lack clarity.

You can bring these tracks inside, by the way, even if you seldom see their owners. Make a sloppy paste of plaster of paris and pour it in the footprint. Wait ten minutes, lift the hardened plaster, and there's your track in reverse, the actual shape of the foot that made it. Such a casting makes an interesting paperweight or conversation piece, even if it's just a squirrel print.

The feeding activities of mammals vary with the species. Mice climb to the top of sumac clusters, nipping the seeds and scattering fragments on the snow. Squirrels clip off tree buds and twigs, both for their edible qualities and for the sap that flows from the wound. You can identify the distinctive cuts made by rabbits and mice and squirrels. Those buck teeth are best used by tipping the head sideways, so the twig is clipped off neatly and on a slant. Mice as well as skunks will remove portions of the bark of young trees—one sign of mammals that is often greeted with less than wild enthusiasm by the homeowner.

If your unofficial zoo is blessed by the presence of a deer, you will find that its feeding signs, too, are characteristic. Deer have no top teeth in front, but could use a set of uppers. They merely clamp down on edible twigs with their lower teeth against a hard pad in the top of the mouth. Or they wrap a prehensile tongue around a twig and give a twist of the head. The result is a frayed, broken end, almost as if the twig had been snapped off by hand.

Foxes trot along with their tracks in almost perfect register: each hind foot lands in the spot just vacated by the corresponding front foot, thus leaving a single trail of prints as if made by a one-legged dog. Cat prints are similarly placed, but they may be spaced at intervals of one foot, while fox prints are about 18 inches apart. And fox prints show claw marks, while the claws of cats are sheathed. Then, too, since a fox is a member of the dog family, he visits stumps and bushes just as a dog visits a fire hydrant. I have often seen where a fox has paused at a spot favored earlier by a brief intermission on the part of a dog; the fox solemnly adds his own signature to the community register.

There are a number of books on tracks and animal signs that can help you discover how well your wildlife program is faring. But the best "book" is the land itself; scratch marks on trees, shrubbery bent and nibbled, little scats marking the brief pause of some woodland creature, old bird nests roofed over by mice or tousled masses of soft material at the base of a grass clump—the home of a mouse or the half-sheltered "form" of a resting rabbit.

In all these outdoor efforts, remember those two requisites of food and shelter. Both are best provided along a boundary that affords a variety of environment in a small space. An overgrown fence row, for instance, combines open field and fruiting bushes (food) with tangles and twigs (shelter). Alders and willows arching over a stream offer the same two basic requirements. That part of a forest that meets a field is a far better provider for wildlife than the deep, unbroken woods. A woodland trail through an otherwise solid stand of trees, or an opening created where some forest giant has fallen, will likewise be frequented by animals.

A well-managed grove or forest offers good living conditions for wildlife. Full-sized trees, when cut for lumber, leave sunny openings on the forest floor. In such openings new plants can sprout—young trees, shrubs, wildflowers. Thus the whole forest benefits along with its wildlife population.

Such a habitat—the combination of two or more kinds of environment in a small space—is more productive than either of these surroundings alone, and is known by wildlife specialists as the "edge effect." Even man enjoys the edge effect. The choicest building lots are on street corners, and many towns are at the confluence of rivers or where rivers empty into large bodies of water. Our vacation spots, too, utilize edges. We put a cottage on the beach or on a mountainside and, if possible, we provide a visual "edge" in the form of a view. We also strive for edges in our back yards. Most people find the combination of garden, lawn and shrubs more attractive than any single one of them alone.

Sometimes the visits of furred neighbors can be overwhelming, like the Hosleys with their skunks, or my daughter Janice and her husband who found a congregation of bats in the attic of an old farmhouse they bought. Even if skunks and bats were here before civilized man, there are limits to their rights. So here, in closing, a word about such situations.

The Hosley skunks did, indeed, follow the food trail out of the cellar—after the Hosleys laid a plank to serve as a ramp up the hatchway steps. Skunks are poor climbers, and seem to be forever falling into places where they cannot get out. A ramp, plus a few edible inducements, usually does the trick. Janice and Steve discouraged the bats by plugging up the holes at night after their unbidden guests had left for the evening. Then they placed several bright electric lights in the attic as a further inducement for the bats to go elsewhere, for these nocturnal creatures prefer dark resting places.

Squirrels in the wall often have to be live-trapped and taken at least five miles away or they will soon return. Peg's mother's summer cottage had a series of unscheduled visits by white-footed mice who filled her shoes with wild cherry pits; they, too, needed the trap-and-transport treatment, but in their case only three miles away. We had to live-trap a skunk, too, after it had puttered its way over a friend's lawn and right into a pit the local well diggers had left partially covered. We hoisted the skunk from its cramped quarters with a sigh of relief and allowed it to go on about its absent-minded amblings in the friend's yard.

But the skunk wasn't the only one that was absent-minded. Congratulating ourselves over our good fortune in releasing the animal without a mishap, Peg and I got in the car without another thought, drove home—and found a message telling us to come rescue the same skunk from the same hole all over again.

That's the way it is with animals. Whether it's an uncommunicative clam, a half-grown baby bird blown out of the nest or a twice-sunk skunk silently eyeing you from eight feet down, living creatures present a challenge—and a reward.

Hopefully, this book has helped to meet the challenge. The rewards will come automatically.

Index

188

189